AutoGen Mastery

Crafting Multi-Agent Systems to Revolutionize Automation and Collaboration

James Acklin

Copyright Page

Table of Contents

Preface

The world is on the brink of a transformative era driven by automation, artificial intelligence, and the seamless collaboration of intelligent systems. As industries evolve to meet the growing demands of efficiency, scalability, and innovation, a new paradigm has emerged at the intersection of these advancements: Multi-Agent Systems (MAS). These systems, composed of independent yet cooperative agents, hold the potential to revolutionize automation, redefine collaboration, and solve complex problems in ways we could only dream of a few decades ago.

The purpose of **AutoGen Mastery: Crafting Multi-Agent Systems to Revolutionize Automation and Collaboration** is to provide a comprehensive guide for understanding, designing, and implementing multi-agent systems that can tackle real-world challenges. Whether you are an academic, a professional in the tech industry, or simply an enthusiast keen to explore the forefront of automation, this book is your gateway to mastering the concepts and practices that underpin MAS.

This book is designed to bridge the gap between theory and practice. It begins with foundational knowledge, introducing key concepts, historical context, and the principles that make multi-agent systems distinct. As you progress, you will delve deeper into the building blocks of MAS, learning about agent design, communication protocols, and the integration of learning algorithms to create adaptive, intelligent systems.

From there, we explore how MAS is transforming industries such as manufacturing, healthcare, transportation, and beyond. Through real-world case studies and examples, you will gain a clear understanding of how MAS are being leveraged to solve pressing challenges. Along the way, we address the ethical, technical, and security considerations that come with deploying these systems in a connected, data-driven world.

For those eager to put their knowledge into practice, this book offers hands-on tutorials, guidance on using popular MAS frameworks, and strategies for deploying systems in diverse environments. We also look ahead to emerging trends such as the integration of MAS with blockchain, artificial intelligence, and quantum computing, offering a glimpse into the future of this dynamic field.

Writing this book has been a journey of discovery and reflection, fueled by the conviction that MAS is not just a technology—it is a framework for collaboration and innovation that can shape the future of humanity. By combining insights from leading research, practical techniques, and visionary ideas, this book seeks to inspire readers to harness the full potential of MAS.

As you embark on this journey, I encourage you to approach the material with curiosity and a mindset of exploration. Multi-agent systems are complex, but their transformative potential is unparalleled. Mastery of this field will not only prepare you to thrive in the era of intelligent automation but also empower you to contribute meaningfully to its evolution.

I hope this book serves as a valuable resource, a source of inspiration, and a guide as you delve into the fascinating world of multi-agent systems. Together, let us explore how we can craft systems that revolutionize automation, enable collaboration, and build a brighter, smarter future.

Chapter 1: Introduction to Multi-Agent Systems

1.1 What Are Multi-Agent Systems?

Multi-agent systems are a concept in computer science and artificial intelligence that involve a collection of independent entities, known as "agents," working together to solve problems, perform tasks, or achieve goals. Each agent has its own set of abilities, knowledge, and decision-making capabilities, allowing it to act autonomously within a system. What makes MAS particularly powerful is the ability of these agents to interact and collaborate in dynamic and often complex environments.

Key Characteristics of Multi-Agent Systems

Autonomy

Each agent operates independently, meaning it does not need constant supervision or input to function. For instance, an agent can perceive its environment, make decisions based on its programming, and act accordingly. This is particularly important when agents are deployed in environments where real-time human intervention is impractical, such as Mars rovers exploring the surface of another planet.

Collaboration

The essence of MAS lies in the way agents work together. Collaboration enables agents to share information, divide tasks, and coordinate actions. This cooperation often results in better outcomes than agents acting in isolation. For example, consider a fleet of autonomous delivery drones. If one drone's battery is low, it can request assistance from another drone to complete a delivery.

Adaptability

Agents in a multi-agent system can respond to changes in their environment. This is crucial in dynamic settings like stock trading platforms, where market conditions can change rapidly.

Decentralization

In MAS, there is no central authority dictating what every agent should do. Instead, decision-making is distributed among the agents. This not only makes the system more robust but also ensures it can handle large-scale operations.

How Agents Work

Agents are at the core of a multi-agent system. An agent can be thought of as a software program (or sometimes a physical entity, like a robot) that is designed to perform specific tasks. To function effectively, an agent must have certain capabilities:

Perception: The ability to sense its environment using sensors or data inputs.

Decision-Making: Logic or algorithms that allow the agent to decide what actions to take.

Action: The ability to perform tasks or execute commands based on its decisions.

Communication: The capacity to interact with other agents or systems to exchange information.

Here's a simple code example of an agent implemented in Python:

class Agent:

```
    def __init__(self, name):
        self.name = name
        self.energy = 100   # Default energy level

    def perceive(self, environment):
        print(f"{self.name} is perceiving the
environment: {environment}")

    def decide(self):
        if self.energy > 50:
            return "perform_task"
        else:
            return "recharge"

    def act(self, decision):
```

```
        if decision == "perform_task":
            print(f"{self.name} is performing a
task.")
            self.energy -= 20
        elif decision == "recharge":
            print(f"{self.name} is recharging.")
            self.energy += 30

# Example usage
environment = "warehouse"
agent = Agent("Robot-1")
agent.perceive(environment)
decision = agent.decide()
agent.act(decision)
```

This simple example represents the core functions of an agent: perceiving the environment, making decisions, and acting. In a more complex system, these agents would interact and collaborate to achieve larger goals.

Real-World Examples of MAS

Smart Grids
In energy distribution, MAS are used to manage and optimize electricity flow between power producers and consumers. Each agent could represent an energy provider, a consumer, or even a device like a smart thermostat. These agents communicate to ensure that electricity is distributed efficiently, reducing energy waste.

Autonomous Vehicles
Self-driving cars rely on MAS principles to operate safely and efficiently. Each car (agent) perceives its surroundings, makes decisions about speed and direction, and communicates with other vehicles to avoid collisions and optimize traffic flow.

Healthcare Systems
In hospitals, MAS can be used to manage resources like operating rooms, medical staff, and equipment. Agents representing patients, doctors, and facilities collaborate to ensure that the right resources are available at the right time.

Why Multi-Agent Systems Matter

The complexity of modern problems often exceeds the capabilities of traditional systems. Centralized solutions can become bottlenecks, especially as scale increases. Multi-agent systems provide a way to distribute complexity, making them scalable, robust, and efficient.

Let's consider disaster management as an example. In a natural disaster, coordination between search-and-rescue teams, supply distribution systems, and first responders is critical. A MAS can represent each team or resource as an agent. These agents communicate and coordinate autonomously, allowing rescue efforts to adapt to rapidly changing conditions without waiting for instructions from a central command.

Exercise: Building a Simple Collaborative MAS

Let's build a simple MAS where two agents collaborate to complete a task: delivering packages.

```python
class DeliveryAgent:
    def __init__(self, name):
        self.name = name
        self.capacity = 5   # Maximum number of
packages the agent can carry
        self.packages_delivered = 0

    def deliver_package(self):
        if self.capacity > 0:
            self.capacity -= 1
            self.packages_delivered += 1
            print(f"{self.name} delivered a
package. Remaining capacity: {self.capacity}")
        else:
            print(f"{self.name} has no capacity
left. Requesting help...")

    def recharge(self):
        self.capacity = 5
        print(f"{self.name} has recharged and is
ready to deliver more packages.")

# Two agents collaborating
```

```
agent1 = DeliveryAgent("Drone-1")
agent2 = DeliveryAgent("Drone-2")

# Delivery process
for i in range(6):   # Simulating 6 package
deliveries
    if agent1.capacity > 0:
        agent1.deliver_package()
    else:
        agent1.recharge()
        agent2.deliver_package()
```

This example shows how agents can handle tasks individually and collaborate when one agent runs out of capacity. It demonstrates the principles of autonomy, communication, and adaptability.

Multi-agent systems represent a powerful shift in how we approach automation and problem-solving. By understanding the core concepts and working through practical examples, you'll be equipped to explore more advanced topics, such as agent communication protocols, coordination strategies, and real-world deployment.

1.2 The Need for Multi-Agent Systems

Multi-agent systems shine in environments where complexity, scale, and adaptability are key. They are not a replacement for traditional systems but an enhancement that allows us to tackle challenges previously out of reach.

Before we dive into why MAS is needed, let's discuss the challenges of centralized systems. A centralized system relies on a single control point to manage everything. Think of it like a conductor leading an orchestra: the conductor tells each musician when to play and what notes to perform. While this works for small groups or simple tasks, it quickly becomes a bottleneck as the size of the group or complexity of the task grows.

Here's why centralized systems struggle in complex environments:

Scalability Issues
A centralized system can only handle so much before it becomes overwhelmed. For example, consider an online store during a big sale event.

A centralized server might crash under heavy traffic because it can't process all the requests simultaneously. With MAS, you could distribute the workload across multiple agents, ensuring smooth operation.

Single Point of Failure

Centralized systems are prone to breakdowns if the central control fails. For example, a power outage at a traffic control center could bring an entire city's traffic to a standstill. In MAS, failure of one agent doesn't collapse the whole system because each agent can continue working independently or adapt.

Lack of Flexibility

Centralized systems follow predefined rules and struggle to adapt to unforeseen circumstances. Consider a centralized delivery system during a natural disaster. If roads are blocked, the central control might fail to reroute deliveries effectively. In contrast, agents in MAS can use local information to adapt their plans.

Unique Benefits of Multi-Agent Systems

Multi-agent systems solve these challenges by distributing control and enabling collaboration. Let's explore the benefits of MAS and how they address real-world needs.

Scalability and Distribution

In MAS, tasks and responsibilities are distributed among multiple agents. Each agent operates independently but collaborates with others to achieve the system's goals. This decentralized approach allows MAS to handle large-scale problems efficiently.

For example, in a warehouse, robots (agents) can divide tasks like sorting, picking, and packing items. Instead of relying on a single central computer to assign tasks, each robot communicates with others to optimize the process.

Here's a simple example in Python to demonstrate a scalable task distribution:

class Agent:

```
    def __init__(self, name):
        self.name = name
```

```
    def perform_task(self, task):
        print(f"{self.name} is performing task:
{task}")

# Distribute tasks among agents
tasks = ["sort items", "pick items", "pack items",
"label boxes"]
agents = [Agent("Robot-1"), Agent("Robot-2"),
Agent("Robot-3")]

for i, task in enumerate(tasks):
    agent = agents[i % len(agents)]   # Assign tasks
in a round-robin manner
    agent.perform_task(task)
```

This simple example shows how tasks can be distributed evenly among multiple agents. In a real-world scenario, agents could also decide task assignments based on availability or proximity.

Fault Tolerance

Since MAS does not rely on a single point of control, it is inherently more robust. If one agent fails, others can take over its tasks. For example, if one drone in a delivery system runs out of battery, another nearby drone can step in to complete the delivery. This adaptability ensures the system continues to function smoothly even when individual components fail.

Let's look at a Python example where agents back each other up in case of failure:

class Delivery Agent:

```
    def __init__(self, name, capacity):
        self.name = name
        self.capacity = capacity

    def deliver(self, package):
        if self.capacity > 0:
            self.capacity -= 1
            print(f"{self.name} delivered
{package}. Remaining capacity: {self.capacity}")
```

```
            return True
        else:
            print(f"{self.name} cannot deliver
{package}. No capacity left.")
            return False

# Simulate delivery with fault tolerance
agent1 = DeliveryAgent("Drone-1", 3)
agent2 = DeliveryAgent("Drone-2", 2)

packages = ["Package-1", "Package-2", "Package-3",
"Package-4", "Package-5"]

for package in packages:
    if not agent1.deliver(package):   # If Drone-1
fails
        agent2.deliver(package)   # Drone-2 takes
over
```

Here, you can see how agents collaborate to handle tasks, ensuring smooth operation even if one agent reaches its limit.

Dynamic and Adaptive Behavior

MAS thrives in environments where conditions change frequently. For instance, in disaster response scenarios, MAS can be used to coordinate rescue efforts. Each agent (e.g., a robot, drone, or vehicle) gathers local information, communicates with others, and adapts to the situation.

In a simulated disaster scenario, MAS might work like this:

Agents explore the area and identify blocked roads, collapsed buildings, or trapped victims.

They share information with nearby agents to update the overall map of the disaster zone.

Based on real-time data, agents decide the best actions to take, such as clearing debris or delivering supplies.

Real-World Applications of MAS

Smart Cities

MAS is the backbone of many smart city applications. For example, traffic management systems use MAS to coordinate traffic lights, optimize public transportation routes, and manage emergency vehicles. Each component (e.g., a traffic light or bus) acts as an agent, sharing data and making local decisions that contribute to the larger goal of reducing congestion.

E-Commerce and Logistics

Companies like Amazon use MAS to manage warehouses filled with robots. Each robot acts as an agent, picking and moving items based on orders. They communicate with one another to avoid collisions and optimize paths, ensuring fast and efficient order fulfillment.

Environmental Monitoring

In wildlife conservation, MAS is used to monitor animal populations. Drones (agents) can survey large areas, share data on wildlife sightings, and identify patterns. This decentralized approach allows researchers to gather more comprehensive and accurate data.

Practical Exercise: Collaborative Agents

Let's create a simple MAS where agents collaborate to complete a series of tasks, ensuring no single agent is overloaded.

class Task Agent:

```
    def __init__(self, name, max_tasks):
        self.name = name
        self.max_tasks = max_tasks
        self.current_tasks = 0

    def can_take_task(self):
        return self.current_tasks < self.max_tasks

    def assign_task(self, task):
        if self.can_take_task():
            self.current_tasks += 1
            print(f"{self.name} is handling task:
{task}")
        else:
            print(f"{self.name} cannot take any
more tasks.")
```

```
# Create agents
agent1 = TaskAgent("Agent-1", 2)
agent2 = TaskAgent("Agent-2", 3)

tasks = ["Task-1", "Task-2", "Task-3", "Task-4",
"Task-5"]

# Assign tasks to agents
for task in tasks:
    if agent1.can_take_task():
        agent1.assign_task(task)
    else:
        agent2.assign_task(task)
```

This example demonstrates how agents can share workloads based on their capacity, showcasing the flexibility and scalability of MAS.

The need for multi-agent systems arises from the growing complexity, scale, and unpredictability of modern problems. By enabling distributed control, adaptability, and collaboration, MAS offers solutions that traditional systems cannot match. Whether it's coordinating autonomous vehicles, managing warehouses, or responding to natural disasters, MAS is shaping the future of intelligent systems. Understanding how these systems operate and implementing them effectively opens up a world of possibilities.

1.3 Historical Context and Trends

To truly understand where multi-agent systems (MAS) are today, it's essential to explore how they have evolved. The journey of MAS is not just about technological progress but also about solving real-world problems in ways that were previously unimaginable. From their roots in distributed artificial intelligence to their role in cutting-edge applications like autonomous vehicles and smart cities, the history of MAS reveals a fascinating progression of ideas and innovation.

Early Beginnings: Distributed Artificial Intelligence

The concept of multi-agent systems emerged in the late 1970s and early 1980s as a branch of distributed artificial intelligence (DAI). DAI sought to address the limitations of centralized AI systems by distributing intelligence across multiple entities. At the time, researchers recognized that solving complex problems often required dividing tasks among multiple components that could work independently yet collaboratively.

One of the earliest breakthroughs was the **Contract Net Protocol** introduced by Reid G. Smith in 1980. This protocol defined a framework for task allocation where agents could negotiate and assign tasks based on their capabilities. Think of it as an auction system: one agent announces a task, and others bid on it based on their availability or expertise. The best-suited agent gets the task, ensuring efficiency and fairness. Even today, this protocol serves as the foundation for many MAS coordination mechanisms.

The 1990s: Formalizing Concepts and Frameworks

As the field grew in the 1990s, researchers began to formalize the principles of MAS. This period saw the introduction of theoretical models and communication protocols that are still influential today. For example, the **Foundation for Intelligent Physical Agents (FIPA)** was established to create standards for agent communication, ensuring interoperability across systems. FIPA's standards allowed agents from different developers or systems to communicate effectively, much like humans speaking a common language.

During this time, the focus shifted to defining what an "agent" should be. Researchers proposed characteristics like autonomy, adaptability, and proactivity. These traits distinguished agents from simple software programs, emphasizing their ability to make decisions independently and respond intelligently to changes in their environment.

Here's a simple example to show how agents began to interact using basic communication protocols:

class Agent:

```
    def __init__(self, name):
        self.name = name

    def send_message(self, recipient, message):
        print(f"{self.name} to {recipient.name}:
{message}")
```

```
    def receive_message(self, sender, message):
        print(f"{self.name} received message from
{sender.name}: {message}")

# Creating agents
agent1 = Agent("Agent-1")
agent2 = Agent("Agent-2")

# Communication example
agent1.send_message(agent2, "Requesting task
status.")
agent2.receive_message(agent1, "Requesting task
status.")
agent2.send_message(agent1, "Task is 50%
complete.")
agent1.receive_message(agent2, "Task is 50%
complete.")
```

This simple code illustrates how agents communicate in a basic MAS. In real systems, these interactions would involve complex protocols and larger-scale coordination.

The Rise of Real-World Applications (2000s)

By the 2000s, MAS was no longer confined to theoretical research—it began to find practical applications in industries like manufacturing, logistics, and robotics. Advances in computing power and network infrastructure allowed MAS to scale and operate in more dynamic environments.

One notable example was the introduction of **swarm robotics**, inspired by the behavior of social insects like ants and bees. In these systems, multiple robots (agents) worked together to achieve a goal, such as searching for objects or building structures. Unlike traditional robotics, swarm robotics emphasized decentralized control, with each robot acting autonomously based on local information.

For instance, consider a system where drones search a disaster zone for survivors. Each drone explores a specific area and shares its findings with others, ensuring no area is left unchecked. This decentralized approach ensures efficiency and robustness, even if some drones fail.

Here's a simple simulation of swarm behavior:

import random

class Drone:

```
    def __init__(self, name, position):
        self.name = name
        self.position = position

    def move(self):
        # Random movement to simulate exploration
        self.position[0] += random.choice([-1, 1])
        self.position[1] += random.choice([-1, 1])

    def report_position(self):
        print(f"{self.name} is at position
{self.position}")

# Create a swarm of drones
drones = [Drone(f"Drone-{i+1}", [0, 0]) for i in
range(5)]

# Simulate movement
for _ in range(5):   # Run for 5 steps
    for drone in drones:
        drone.move()
        drone.report_position()
```

In this example, each drone explores its environment independently, simulating how swarm systems work in the real world.

Current Trends: The Integration of MAS with Emerging Technologies

Today, MAS is at the forefront of innovation, driving advancements in areas like artificial intelligence, blockchain, and the Internet of Things (IoT).

Artificial Intelligence and Learning Agents

Modern MAS increasingly integrate machine learning to create agents that learn from their experiences. For example, self-driving cars rely on MAS principles to navigate roads, avoid collisions, and coordinate with other vehicles. Each car acts as an agent, processing local data and sharing critical information with others to ensure safety.

Blockchain for Trust and Security

Blockchain technology is being used in MAS to ensure secure and transparent interactions between agents. In supply chain management, MAS can track goods as they move through the chain. Each agent logs its actions on the blockchain, creating an immutable record that ensures accountability.

IoT and Smart Environments

MAS powers many smart environments, such as homes, factories, and cities. In a smart home, agents representing devices like thermostats, lights, and appliances collaborate to optimize energy use and enhance convenience.

For example, if a thermostat detects that a room is empty, it can communicate with the lights to turn them off, saving energy. Here's a basic example of IoT-style agent communication:

class Device Agent:

```
    def __init__(self, name):
        self.name = name
        self.status = "off"

    def update_status(self, new_status):
        self.status = new_status
        print(f"{self.name} status updated to
{self.status}")

# Create device agents
thermostat = DeviceAgent("Thermostat")
light = DeviceAgent("Light")

# Collaboration example
if thermostat.status == "off":
    light.update_status("off")
```

This type of coordination is just the beginning of what MAS can achieve in IoT systems.

The Future of MAS

The field of MAS is evolving rapidly, and the future promises even greater possibilities. Emerging trends include:

Quantum Computing: Exploring how MAS can leverage quantum algorithms for faster problem-solving.

Edge Computing: Enabling agents to process data locally, reducing latency and improving performance.

Human-Agent Collaboration: Creating systems where agents assist humans more intuitively, enhancing productivity and decision-making.

As we continue to push the boundaries of technology, MAS will play an essential role in solving some of the world's most pressing challenges.

The history of multi-agent systems is a story of innovation and adaptability. From their roots in distributed artificial intelligence to their role in modern applications, MAS has evolved into a critical technology for tackling complex, dynamic problems. By understanding their historical context and current trends, you can appreciate the transformative potential of MAS and how they are shaping the future.

Chapter 2: Foundations of Multi-Agent Systems

The foundation of multi-agent systems (MAS) lies in understanding their core concepts, how they are structured, and the principles guiding their design. In this chapter, we'll explore the essential building blocks of MAS, how agents interact within different architectures, and the design principles that make these systems robust, efficient, and scalable. Let's take it step by step, making sure everything is clear and practical.

2.1 Core Concepts of MAS

Multi-agent systems (MAS) are an exciting field of computer science and artificial intelligence that revolve around creating systems made up of multiple interacting agents. Each agent is autonomous and intelligent in its own right, and together they work to solve problems, achieve goals, or perform tasks. To truly grasp the power and potential of MAS, we need to break down its core concepts.

An agent is the fundamental unit of a multi-agent system. Think of an agent as a software entity that acts independently within an environment to achieve specific goals. It perceives its surroundings, makes decisions, and takes actions. Importantly, agents can be anything from a simple script that monitors server status to a sophisticated robot navigating a warehouse.

Here's a way to visualize an agent in practical terms:

Perception: The agent senses data from its environment. For example, a drone might detect weather conditions or a warehouse robot might scan for packages.

Decision-making: Based on its goals and the data it perceives, the agent decides on the best course of action.

Action: The agent executes its decision, such as moving to a specific location or sending a message to another agent.

Here's a simple code representation of an agent in Python:

class Agent:

```
def __init__(self, name, goal):
    self.name = name
    self.goal = goal

def perceive(self, environment):
    print(f"{self.name} perceives:
{environment}")

def decide(self, observation):
    if observation == "task available":
        return "perform task"
    return "standby"

def act(self, decision):
    print(f"{self.name} is acting: {decision}")

# Example of an agent in action
environment = "task available"
agent = Agent("Robot-1", "Complete assigned tasks")
agent.perceive(environment)
decision = agent.decide(environment)
agent.act(decision)
```

In this example, the agent perceives its environment, decides what to do based on the observed conditions, and acts accordingly. While this is a basic agent, more advanced agents may include machine learning algorithms to improve decision-making.

Autonomy

One of the defining features of an agent is autonomy. Autonomy means that an agent can operate independently, without requiring constant oversight or instructions. This is critical for applications like autonomous vehicles or distributed systems, where centralized control would be inefficient or impossible.

For example, think about a thermostat. A smart thermostat doesn't need you to adjust it every time the temperature changes. It senses the room temperature and adjusts itself to meet a target temperature. This independence is autonomy in action.

Environment

Every agent exists within an environment. The environment could be a physical space, like a factory floor, or a virtual space, like an e-commerce platform. The environment provides the agent with data and context for its actions. It may also impose constraints, such as physical barriers for a robot or limited resources for an optimization problem.

In MAS, environments can be:

Static or Dynamic: A static environment doesn't change much, while a dynamic environment, like traffic, changes constantly.

Fully Observable or Partially Observable: In a fully observable environment, agents have access to all relevant data. In a partially observable environment, agents must make decisions with incomplete information.

Here's an example of an agent interacting with a simple environment:

class Simple Environment:

```
    def __init__(self, state):
        self.state = state

    def get_state(self):
        return self.state

class Agent:
    def __init__(self, name):
        self.name = name

    def act(self, environment):
        state = environment.get_state()
        if state == "obstacle":
            print(f"{self.name} avoids the
obstacle.")
        else:
            print(f"{self.name} continues
forward.")

# Simulating an agent in an environment
env = SimpleEnvironment("obstacle")
robot = Agent("Robot-1")
```

```
robot.act(env)
```

This interaction shows how the environment influences an agent's decisions and actions.

Communication

In a multi-agent system, agents rarely work in isolation. They need to communicate to share information, coordinate tasks, and negotiate solutions. Communication is a key aspect of MAS that allows agents to function as a cohesive system.

For example, in a team of delivery drones, one drone might inform others about obstacles or request assistance when its battery is low. The ability to share this information ensures efficiency and adaptability.

Here's an example of two agents communicating:

class Communicating Agent:

```
    def __init__(self, name):
        self.name = name

    def send_message(self, recipient, message):
        print(f"{self.name} to {recipient.name}:
{message}")

    def receive_message(self, sender, message):
        print(f"{self.name} received from
{sender.name}: {message}")

# Creating agents
agent1 = CommunicatingAgent("Agent-1")
agent2 = CommunicatingAgent("Agent-2")

# Communication example
agent1.send_message(agent2, "Need assistance with
Task A")
agent2.receive_message(agent1, "Need assistance
with Task A")
```

This basic exchange shows how agents can communicate in a structured way. In real-world applications, communication protocols are often more complex, involving standards like FIPA (Foundation for Intelligent Physical Agents).

Collaboration and Coordination

When multiple agents work together, coordination is essential. Agents must allocate tasks, share resources, and avoid conflicts. Effective coordination ensures that the system operates efficiently and achieves its overall goals.

For instance, in a warehouse, robots (agents) must avoid collisions while working together to fulfill orders. If one robot is closer to an item, it might inform others that it will handle that task, avoiding redundancy.

Here's an example of collaborative task allocation:

class Collaborative Agent:

```
    def __init__(self, name):
        self.name = name
        self.task = None

    def assign_task(self, task):
        if not self.task:
            self.task = task
            print(f"{self.name} is assigned task:
{task}")
        else:
            print(f"{self.name} is already busy
with task: {self.task}")

# Simulating task assignment
agent1 = CollaborativeAgent("Agent-1")
agent2 = CollaborativeAgent("Agent-2")

tasks = ["Pick item A", "Deliver item B"]

for task in tasks:
    if not agent1.task:
        agent1.assign_task(task)
    else:
        agent2.assign_task(task)
```

This demonstrates how agents can coordinate task allocation to optimize their workload.

Learning and Adaptability

Some agents are designed to learn from their experiences and adapt to changing environments. This capability is particularly important in dynamic environments, where conditions can change unpredictably. Machine learning algorithms, such as reinforcement learning, are often used to enable this adaptability.

For example, a robot vacuum cleaner learns the layout of your home over time, optimizing its cleaning path and avoiding obstacles more effectively.

Here's a simple illustration of an agent adapting to feedback:

class Learning Agent:

```
    def __init__(self, name):
        self.name = name
        self.success_count = 0

    def learn(self, result):
        if result == "success":
            self.success_count += 1
            print(f"{self.name} learned from
success. Total successes: {self.success_count}")
        else:
            print(f"{self.name} learned from
failure.")

# Simulating a learning process
agent = LearningAgent("Agent-1")
outcomes = ["success", "failure", "success"]

for outcome in outcomes:
    agent.learn(outcome)
```

This shows how agents can adapt based on feedback, improving their performance over time.

The core concepts of MAS—agents, autonomy, environments, communication, collaboration, and learning—are the foundation of this powerful field. By understanding how these elements work together, you gain insight into the design and operation of multi-agent systems. These systems are not just theoretical constructs; they address real-world challenges, from automating logistics to managing smart cities. The examples and code snippets provided here give you a practical understanding of these concepts, paving the way for deeper exploration into MAS.

2.2 Architectures of Multi-Agent Systems

To understand how multi-agent systems (MAS) work, it's important to grasp their architecture. The architecture of a MAS defines how agents are organized, interact, and make decisions. It's the blueprint that determines how the system functions, how data flows between agents, and how tasks are coordinated. A well-designed architecture ensures that the system is robust, efficient, and scalable.

The Basics of MAS Architecture

At its core, an MAS architecture defines the relationship between agents and their environment. This includes:

How agents communicate with each other.

How tasks are assigned and coordinated.

How decisions are made—whether centrally, independently, or through negotiation.

How failures are handled to ensure the system remains functional.

The architecture of an MAS is influenced by the problem it's designed to solve. For instance, a system managing air traffic would have a different structure than one coordinating robots in a warehouse. Let's explore the three primary types of MAS architectures: **centralized**, **decentralized**, and **hybrid**.

Centralized Architectures

In a centralized architecture, there is a single central entity or agent responsible for managing and coordinating all other agents. The central agent acts as the "brain" of the system, making decisions and assigning tasks to the individual agents.

How It Works

The central agent collects information from all other agents.

It processes this information and decides what each agent should do.

Agents execute tasks as instructed by the central agent and report their results back.

This setup is straightforward and easy to implement, as the logic is concentrated in one place.

Real-World Example

Consider a warehouse where a central system assigns robots to pick up items from shelves. The central system knows where each robot is, where the items are located, and which orders need to be fulfilled. Based on this information, it dispatches robots to complete the tasks.

Advantages

Simple to design and debug.

Centralized control ensures consistency.

Easy to monitor and manage.

Disadvantages

A single point of failure: If the central agent goes down, the entire system stops.

Limited scalability: As the number of agents increases, the central agent becomes a bottleneck.

Code Example: Centralized Task Assignment

```
class CentralAgent:
    def __init__(self):
        self.agents = []

    def register_agent(self, agent):
```

```
        self.agents.append(agent)

    def assign_tasks(self, tasks):
        for task, agent in zip(tasks, self.agents):
            agent.perform_task(task)

class Agent:
    def __init__(self, name):
        self.name = name

    def perform_task(self, task):
        print(f"{self.name} is performing task:
{task}")

# Setup
central_agent = CentralAgent()
agent1 = Agent("Agent-1")
agent2 = Agent("Agent-2")

central_agent.register_agent(agent1)
central_agent.register_agent(agent2)

tasks = ["Pick item A", "Deliver item B"]
central_agent.assign_tasks(tasks)
```

In this example, the central agent assigns tasks to individual agents, showcasing centralized control.

Decentralized Architectures

A decentralized architecture distributes decision-making among the agents themselves. There is no central entity controlling the system; instead, each agent operates autonomously and collaborates with others to achieve the system's goals.

How It Works

Each agent has its own decision-making capabilities.

Agents communicate with each other to share information and coordinate actions.

Decisions are made locally based on the agent's environment and goals.

Real-World Example

In traffic management, each traffic light can act as an agent, operating autonomously based on local traffic conditions. Lights communicate with neighboring lights to optimize traffic flow without relying on a central control system.

Advantages

Scalability: More agents can be added without overwhelming a central system.

Robustness: The system continues to function even if some agents fail.

Flexibility: Agents can adapt to local conditions.

Disadvantages

Coordination can be challenging in highly complex systems.

Requires sophisticated communication and decision-making algorithms.

Code Example: Decentralized Decision-Making

```
class DecentralizedAgent:
    def __init__(self, name):
        self.name = name

    def decide(self, environment):
        if environment == "task available":
            print(f"{self.name} is performing the
task.")
        else:
            print(f"{self.name} is idle.")

# Simulating multiple agents
agents = [DecentralizedAgent(f"Agent-{i+1}") for i
in range(3)]
environments = ["task available", "no task", "task
available"]

for agent, environment in zip(agents,
environments):
```

```
agent.decide(environment)
```

Here, each agent makes its own decision based on its local environment, illustrating decentralized control.

Hybrid Architectures

Hybrid architectures combine elements of both centralized and decentralized approaches. In this setup, a central entity may handle high-level planning or coordination, while individual agents operate autonomously to execute specific tasks.

How It Works

The central entity provides guidance or assigns broad goals.

Agents retain autonomy to decide how to achieve their specific tasks.

Coordination between agents and the central entity ensures system-wide consistency.

Real-World Example

In disaster response scenarios, a central command center might assign areas for search-and-rescue operations, but individual teams (agents) decide how to conduct their searches based on local conditions.

Advantages

Balances scalability with centralized oversight.

Maintains robustness and adaptability.

Suitable for complex, dynamic environments.

Disadvantages

More complex to design and implement.

Requires careful coordination between centralized and decentralized components.

Code Example: Hybrid Task Management

```
class CentralCoordinator:
```

```python
    def __init__(self):
        self.agents = []

    def register_agent(self, agent):
        self.agents.append(agent)

    def assign_area(self, areas):
        for area, agent in zip(areas, self.agents):
            agent.set_area(area)

class AutonomousAgent:
    def __init__(self, name):
        self.name = name
        self.area = None

    def set_area(self, area):
        self.area = area

    def operate(self):
        print(f"{self.name} is operating in area:
{self.area}")

# Setup
coordinator = CentralCoordinator()
agent1 = AutonomousAgent("Agent-1")
agent2 = AutonomousAgent("Agent-2")

coordinator.register_agent(agent1)
coordinator.register_agent(agent2)

areas = ["North Zone", "South Zone"]
coordinator.assign_area(areas)

# Autonomous operation
for agent in [agent1, agent2]:
    agent.operate()
```

This hybrid example shows how a central coordinator assigns areas, while agents operate autonomously within their zones.

The choice of architecture depends on the problem being addressed. Centralized systems work well for smaller, simpler problems, while decentralized systems excel in large-scale, dynamic environments. Hybrid systems are ideal for balancing scalability and oversight in complex scenarios.

Understanding the architectures of multi-agent systems is crucial for designing systems that are effective, scalable, and robust. Whether centralized, decentralized, or hybrid, each architecture has its strengths and weaknesses, making it suitable for different applications. By mastering these concepts and applying them thoughtfully, you can build MAS that solve real-world problems with precision and efficiency.

2.3 Design Principles

Designing a multi-agent system (MAS) is much more than simply creating a collection of interacting agents. It's about ensuring the system is efficient, scalable, robust, and capable of achieving its goals, even in dynamic and unpredictable environments. Whether you're working on an MAS for autonomous vehicles, warehouse robots, or smart grids, certain foundational principles guide the process to ensure success. In this section, we'll explore these principles in detail, complete with practical examples and real-world applications to ground your understanding.

1. Modularity and Independence

Modularity is one of the most critical principles in MAS design. Each agent should be designed as a modular, self-contained entity that can operate independently. This independence allows agents to function without requiring constant interaction or control, making the system more scalable and adaptable.

Why It's Important

If one agent fails or is removed, the rest of the system should continue functioning. This modularity also simplifies maintenance and updates, as you can modify or replace one agent without disrupting the entire system.

Real-World Example

In a robotic warehouse, each robot operates as an independent agent. If one robot malfunctions, the others continue their tasks, ensuring minimal disruption.

Code Example: Modular Agents

Here's an example of creating modular agents:

class Agent:

```
    def __init__(self, name, task):
        self.name = name
        self.task = task

    def perform_task(self):
        print(f"{self.name} is performing task:
{self.task}")

# Create independent agents
agent1 = Agent("Robot-1", "Pick items")
agent2 = Agent("Robot-2", "Deliver packages")

# Each agent operates independently
agent1.perform_task()
agent2.perform_task()
```

This shows how each agent is designed to perform its task without dependencies on others.

2. Scalability

As the size of a system grows, it must remain efficient. An MAS should handle the addition of new agents or tasks without a significant drop in performance. Scalability is particularly important in systems with dynamic agent populations, such as IoT networks or autonomous vehicle fleets.

Practical Considerations

Ensure agents communicate efficiently to prevent bottlenecks.

Avoid centralized control that can limit scalability.

Exercise: Simulating Scalability

Here's an example of a system that scales as more agents are added:

class Scalable Agent:

```
def __init__(self, name):
    self.name = name

def act(self):
    print(f"{self.name} is acting.")

# Create a scalable system
agents = [ScalableAgent(f"Agent-{i}") for i in
range(100)]   # Simulating 100 agents

# All agents perform their tasks
for agent in agents:
    agent.act()
```

In this example, the system remains efficient as agents are added, illustrating scalability.

3. Robustness

Robustness ensures the system can handle failures gracefully. This is especially important in decentralized architectures, where individual agent failures should not lead to system-wide collapse.

Real-World Example

In disaster response scenarios, drones coordinate to map affected areas. If one drone loses connection, others take over its assigned zone.

Code Example: Handling Failures

Here's a simplified example of agents compensating for a failure:

class Resilient Agent:

```
def __init__(self, name):
    self.name = name
    self.active = True

def perform_task(self):
    if self.active:
        print(f"{self.name} is performing its
task.")
    else:
```

```
        print(f"{self.name} is inactive.")

# Simulate failure handling
agents = [ResilientAgent(f"Agent-{i}") for i in
range(3)]
agents[1].active = False   # Simulating a failure in
Agent-2

for agent in agents:
    agent.perform_task()
```

This demonstrates how the system adapts when an agent fails, maintaining functionality.

4. Communication and Coordination

In MAS, communication is the glue that holds everything together. Agents need to exchange information, negotiate tasks, and synchronize actions. Effective communication protocols are vital to avoid miscommunication or unnecessary delays.

Challenges

Latency: Communication delays can affect real-time systems.

Overhead: Excessive communication can overwhelm the system.

Real-World Example

In traffic management, autonomous vehicles communicate with each other to optimize routes and avoid collisions. Efficient coordination ensures smooth traffic flow.

Code Example: Coordinating Agents

Here's how agents can communicate and coordinate:

class Communicating Agent:

```
    def __init__(self, name):
        self.name = name

    def send_message(self, recipient, message):
```

```
        print(f"{self.name} to {recipient.name}:
{message}")

    def receive_message(self, sender, message):
        print(f"{self.name} received message from
{sender.name}: {message}")

# Simulate communication
agent1 = CommunicatingAgent("Agent-1")
agent2 = CommunicatingAgent("Agent-2")

agent1.send_message(agent2, "Requesting assistance
with Task A")
agent2.receive_message(agent1, "Requesting
assistance with Task A")
```

This basic communication illustrates how agents exchange information to achieve coordination.

5. Adaptability

In dynamic environments, MAS must adapt to changing conditions. This adaptability often involves agents learning from their experiences or updating their strategies in response to new data.

Real-World Example

In a smart grid, energy management agents adapt to fluctuations in energy supply and demand to maintain stability.

Code Example: Adaptive Agents

Here's an agent that adapts based on feedback:

class Adaptive Agent:

```
    def __init__(self, name):
        self.name = name
        self.energy_level = 100

    def adapt(self, condition):
        if condition == "low energy":
```

```
            self.energy_level += 20
            print(f"{self.name} is adapting:
Recharging. Energy level: {self.energy_level}")
        else:
            print(f"{self.name} is operating
normally.")

# Simulate adaptation
agent = AdaptiveAgent("Agent-1")
agent.adapt("low energy")
agent.adapt("normal")
```

This demonstrates how agents can adjust their behavior based on environmental feedback.

6. Interoperability

In systems where agents are developed by different teams or organizations, interoperability is crucial. Agents must communicate and collaborate seamlessly, regardless of differences in design or programming languages.

Practical Tip

Use standardized protocols like FIPA (Foundation for Intelligent Physical Agents) to ensure compatibility.

7. Transparency and Accountability

In systems with human interaction, agents must be transparent in their decision-making and accountable for their actions. This is particularly important in fields like healthcare, finance, or autonomous driving, where mistakes can have significant consequences.

Real-World Example

In a medical diagnosis system, agents must explain their recommendations clearly to doctors and patients.

Code Example: Logging Agent Decisions

Here's an example of maintaining transparency:

class Transparent Agent:

```python
def __init__(self, name):
    self.name = name

def log_decision(self, decision):
    print(f"{self.name}: Decision logged -
{decision}")

# Simulate decision logging
agent = TransparentAgent("Agent-1")
agent.log_decision("Assigned task to Agent-2")
```

This simple logging ensures transparency in the agent's actions.

Designing a multi-agent system requires careful consideration of principles like modularity, scalability, robustness, communication, adaptability, and transparency. By adhering to these principles, you can create systems that are efficient, resilient, and capable of tackling real-world challenges. The examples provided here offer a practical foundation for applying these concepts, helping you build MAS that meet the demands of today's dynamic and interconnected world.

Chapter 3: Building Blocks of Multi-Agent Systems

To truly understand multi-agent systems (MAS), it's essential to explore their building blocks. These fundamental elements determine how agents are designed, how they interact, and how they learn and adapt. In this chapter, we'll discuss **agent design and behaviors**, **communication and coordination mechanisms**, and **learning and adaptation**—the cornerstones of an effective MAS. By the end, you'll have a comprehensive understanding of how these pieces come together to create intelligent and collaborative systems.

3.1 Agent Design and Behaviors

An agent is more than just a program—it is an autonomous entity capable of perceiving its environment, making decisions, and acting to achieve specific goals. How an agent is designed directly determines its effectiveness and how well it fits within the broader system. Designing an agent involves understanding its behaviors, capabilities, and decision-making processes, ensuring that it operates efficiently in its environment.

An agent must have certain key features to function effectively in a multi-agent system. These features define its interaction with the environment and other agents. Let's break this down:

Perception:
The agent must be able to sense its environment. This could be physical sensors, like a robot detecting obstacles, or virtual inputs, like a program analyzing data from a server.

Decision-Making:
The agent needs logic to interpret what it perceives and determine the best action to take. Decision-making could range from simple rules to advanced machine learning models.

Action:
After deciding what to do, the agent must act. Actions depend on the agent's goals and could involve moving, sending messages, or updating data.

Goals:

Agents are goal-oriented. Whether it's delivering a package, optimizing traffic, or balancing energy usage, every agent works toward achieving specific objectives.

Agent Design in Practice

When designing an agent, the first step is to understand the problem the agent is solving. For example, if you're designing a warehouse robot, the agent's purpose might be to locate, pick, and deliver items. Once the purpose is clear, you can define the agent's behavior.

Reactive and Deliberative Agents

Agents generally fall into two categories based on their behavior:

Reactive Agents:

These agents respond directly to environmental changes. They're fast and straightforward but don't plan ahead. A good analogy is a thermostat that reacts to temperature changes by switching heating or cooling on or off.

Deliberative Agents:

These agents take a more thoughtful approach, considering multiple factors before deciding on an action. For example, a delivery drone might calculate the most efficient route before starting its journey.

Designing a Reactive Agent

Let's design a simple reactive agent in Python. This agent senses whether an obstacle is present and acts accordingly.

class Reactive Agent:

```python
def __init__(self, name):
    self.name = name

def perceive(self, environment):
    return environment.get("obstacle", False)

def act(self, obstacle_detected):
    if obstacle_detected:
```

```
            print(f"{self.name}: Obstacle detected.
Stopping.")
        else:
            print(f"{self.name}: No obstacles.
Moving forward.")

# Simulate environment and agent behavior
environment = {"obstacle": True}
agent = ReactiveAgent("Robot-1")

# Perception and action
obstacle_detected = agent.perceive(environment)
agent.act(obstacle_detected)
```

In this example:

The agent perceives its environment to check for obstacles.

It decides how to act based on what it perceives.

The behavior is immediate and reactive, with no long-term planning.

Designing a Deliberative Agent

Now let's consider a deliberative agent. This agent plans its actions by evaluating its environment and goal before deciding what to do.

class Deliberative Agent:

```
    def __init__(self, name):
        self.name = name
        self.position = 0
        self.goal = 10

    def perceive(self, environment):
        self.obstacle = environment.get("obstacle",
False)

    def decide(self):
        if self.obstacle:
            return "reroute"
        elif self.position < self.goal:
            return "move forward"
```

```
        else:
            return "stop"

    def act(self, decision):
        if decision == "reroute":
            print(f"{self.name}: Obstacle detected.
Rerouting...")
        elif decision == "move forward":
            self.position += 1
            print(f"{self.name}: Moving forward to
position {self.position}.")
        elif decision == "stop":
            print(f"{self.name}: Reached goal.
Stopping.")

# Simulate environment and agent behavior
environment = {"obstacle": False}
agent = DeliberativeAgent("Drone-1")

while agent.position < agent.goal:
    agent.perceive(environment)
    decision = agent.decide()
    agent.act(decision)
```

In this example:

The agent evaluates its current state and the environment before deciding on the best course of action.

It shows deliberate, planned behavior aimed at achieving its goal.

Behavioral Design Patterns

Agents often exhibit specific behavioral patterns based on their purpose. Here are two common patterns:

Goal-Oriented Behavior:
 An agent prioritizes achieving a predefined goal, adjusting its actions as needed. For instance, a robot might pause its task to recharge its battery, ensuring it can complete its primary goal.

Event-Driven Behavior:

The agent's actions are triggered by specific events in the environment. For example, a security camera might start recording when it detects motion.

Exercise: Combining Multiple Behaviors

Let's create an agent that switches between goal-oriented and event-driven behaviors.

class Multi-Behavior Agent:

```python
    def __init__(self, name):
        self.name = name
        self.energy = 100
        self.position = 0
        self.goal = 10

    def perceive(self, environment):
        self.low_energy =
environment.get("low_energy", False)
        self.obstacle = environment.get("obstacle",
False)

    def decide(self):
        if self.low_energy:
            return "recharge"
        elif self.obstacle:
            return "reroute"
        elif self.position < self.goal:
            return "move forward"
        else:
            return "stop"

    def act(self, decision):
        if decision == "recharge":
            self.energy = 100
            print(f"{self.name}: Recharging. Energy
is now {self.energy}.")
        elif decision == "reroute":
            print(f"{self.name}: Obstacle detected.
Finding a new path...")
        elif decision == "move forward":
            self.position += 1
```

```
            self.energy -= 10
            print(f"{self.name}: Moving forward to
position {self.position}. Energy: {self.energy}")
        elif decision == "stop":
            print(f"{self.name}: Reached goal.
Stopping.")

# Simulate environment and agent behavior
environment = {"low_energy": False, "obstacle":
False}
agent = MultiBehaviorAgent("Hybrid-Agent")

while agent.position < agent.goal:
    if agent.energy < 20:
        environment["low_energy"] = True
    else:
        environment["low_energy"] = False

    agent.perceive(environment)
    decision = agent.decide()
    agent.act(decision)
```

This agent demonstrates:

Switching between different behaviors based on the environment and internal state.

A practical approach to handling dynamic situations in real-world systems.

Real-World Applications of Agent Design

Logistics and Delivery

Agents are widely used in logistics to optimize operations. For example, Amazon's warehouse robots are designed to navigate warehouses, avoid collisions, and pick items efficiently. These robots demonstrate both reactive and deliberative behaviors, depending on their tasks and obstacles.

Smart Homes

In a smart home, agents control devices like thermostats, lights, and security systems. These agents communicate and coordinate to create a seamless user experience, balancing energy efficiency and comfort.

Agent design and behavior are foundational to building effective multi-agent systems. By carefully designing how agents perceive, decide, and act, you can create systems that operate efficiently in dynamic environments. Whether reactive, deliberative, or a combination of both, an agent's behavior defines its role and impact within the system.

3.2 Communication and Coordination Mechanisms

In a multi-agent system (MAS), agents rarely work in isolation. Communication and coordination are the lifelines that allow agents to function as a team, sharing information, aligning their goals, and dividing tasks efficiently. Without these mechanisms, agents would act independently, leading to conflicts, inefficiencies, and, in many cases, failure to achieve the system's objectives.

Communication is how agents exchange information to achieve a shared understanding. Whether it's sending a simple message or negotiating a complex agreement, communication is essential for collaboration. There are two primary types of communication in MAS:

Direct Communication: Agents send messages to one another explicitly. For instance, one robot might send a request to another for help with a task.

Indirect Communication: Agents use their environment to communicate, often referred to as **stigmergy**. A good example is how ants leave pheromone trails to guide others to a food source.

In MAS, direct communication is the most common, as it allows for more structured and specific interactions.

Key Components of Agent Communication

Message Protocols: These define the format and structure of messages. A protocol ensures that agents understand each other, even if they are developed independently.

Message Content: This includes the actual data being exchanged, such as requests, responses, or task updates.

Communication Medium: The channel through which messages are sent, such as a network or shared memory.

Code Example: Basic Agent Communication

Let's create two agents that exchange messages about task completion:

class Agent:

```
    def __init__(self, name):
        self.name = name

    def send_message(self, recipient, message):
        print(f"{self.name} to {recipient.name}:
{message}")
        recipient.receive_message(self, message)

    def receive_message(self, sender, message):
        print(f"{self.name} received from
{sender.name}: {message}")

# Creating agents
agent1 = Agent("Agent-1")
agent2 = Agent("Agent-2")

# Communication example
agent1.send_message(agent2, "Task A is complete.")
agent2.send_message(agent1, "Acknowledged. Moving
to Task B.")
```

This example demonstrates how agents can exchange messages. While simplistic, this forms the basis for more complex communication mechanisms.

Coordination in MAS

Coordination is the process of aligning the actions of multiple agents to achieve a shared goal. Without coordination, agents might duplicate efforts, conflict over resources, or work at cross-purposes. Effective coordination ensures that agents work efficiently and harmoniously.

Coordination Mechanisms

Task Allocation:
Agents distribute tasks among themselves based on their capabilities or availability. For instance, in a warehouse, robots might allocate picking, packing, and delivery tasks dynamically.

Negotiation:
Agents negotiate to resolve conflicts or optimize resource usage. For example, two drones might negotiate to determine which one will handle an urgent delivery.

Consensus Building:
In some systems, agents need to agree on a shared goal or decision. This is common in applications like decentralized voting systems.

Leader-Follower Models:
One agent takes on a leadership role, directing others. This approach is often used in swarm robotics or drone formations.

Code Example: Task Allocation

Here's an example where agents coordinate to divide tasks:

class Task Agent:

```
    def __init__(self, name):
        self.name = name
        self.task = None

    def assign_task(self, task):
        if not self.task:
            self.task = task
            print(f"{self.name} is assigned task:
{task}")
        else:
            print(f"{self.name} is already working
on task: {self.task}")
```

```
# Simulating task allocation
tasks = ["Pick item A", "Deliver item B", "Sort
items"]
agents = [TaskAgent(f"Agent-{i}") for i in
range(2)]

# Distribute tasks
for i, task in enumerate(tasks):
    agents[i % len(agents)].assign_task(task)
```

In this example:

Tasks are distributed among agents in a round-robin fashion.

Agents independently decide whether they can take on a new task based on their current workload.

Challenges in Communication and Coordination

While communication and coordination are essential, they come with challenges that need to be addressed:

Scalability: As the number of agents increases, the system must handle the growing volume of messages and coordination complexity without slowing down.

Latency: Delays in communication can impact real-time systems, such as traffic management or emergency response.

Conflict Resolution: When multiple agents compete for the same resource, conflicts must be resolved efficiently to prevent deadlock or inefficiency.

Security: In systems where agents exchange sensitive data, communication must be secure to prevent unauthorized access or tampering.

Real-World Example: Traffic Management

In a smart city, traffic lights can act as agents, communicating with each other to optimize traffic flow. For example:

A traffic light detects heavy congestion at an intersection.

It communicates with neighboring lights to extend green light durations in the affected direction.

Together, the traffic lights coordinate to reduce congestion across the network.

This scenario highlights the importance of both communication and coordination in solving complex, real-world problems.

Exercise: Coordinating Agents to Avoid Conflict

Let's create a system where two agents coordinate to avoid working on the same task simultaneously:

class Coordinating Agent:

```
    def __init__(self, name):
        self.name = name
        self.current_task = None

    def request_task(self, task, shared_tasks):
        if task not in shared_tasks:
            shared_tasks.add(task)
            self.current_task = task
            print(f"{self.name} is assigned task:
{task}")
        else:
            print(f"{self.name} cannot take task:
{task} (already assigned).")

# Shared task tracker
shared_tasks = set()

# Creating agents
agent1 = CoordinatingAgent("Agent-1")
agent2 = CoordinatingAgent("Agent-2")

# Request tasks
agent1.request_task("Task A", shared_tasks)
agent2.request_task("Task A", shared_tasks)
agent2.request_task("Task B", shared_tasks)
```

This example shows:

How agents coordinate to avoid task conflicts.

The use of shared data (in this case, a set) to track task assignments.

Communication and coordination are the backbone of any successful multi-agent system. By enabling agents to share information, resolve conflicts, and align their actions, these mechanisms unlock the full potential of MAS. Whether it's robots working in a warehouse, autonomous vehicles managing traffic, or drones collaborating on a rescue mission, the principles covered here are universally applicable. The provided examples and exercises give you the tools to implement these concepts in your own MAS projects, ensuring they are efficient, scalable, and effective in achieving their goals.

3.3 Learning and Adaptation in Multi-Agent Systems

Learning and adaptation are critical components of multi-agent systems (MAS). They transform static systems into dynamic ones capable of handling evolving environments and unpredictable changes. In an MAS, agents that can learn from past experiences and adapt their behaviors in response to changing conditions are more effective, flexible, and robust. This capability ensures the system remains functional and efficient, even in complex or unforeseen situations.

Learning in MAS involves agents improving their performance over time by analyzing their past actions and their consequences. This process enables agents to make better decisions, achieve goals more efficiently, and adapt to new challenges.

An agent's learning process can be broadly categorized into three types:

Supervised Learning: The agent is trained on labeled datasets, where it learns the correct output for given inputs.

Unsupervised Learning: The agent identifies patterns and relationships in unlabeled data.

Reinforcement Learning (RL): The agent learns through interaction with its environment, receiving rewards or penalties based on its actions.

While all three approaches are valuable, reinforcement learning is particularly relevant for MAS because agents interact directly with their environment and must adapt in real time.

Reinforcement Learning in MAS

Reinforcement learning enables an agent to learn by trial and error. It involves three key elements:

State: The agent's current situation or observation of the environment.

Action: The decision or behavior the agent chooses to perform.

Reward: Feedback indicating the success or failure of the action taken.

The agent's goal is to maximize its cumulative rewards over time.

Code Example: A Simple Reinforcement Learning Agent

Here's an example of a basic agent using reinforcement learning to navigate a grid and reach a goal:

import random

class RLAgent:

```
    def __init__(self, name, grid_size):
        self.name = name
        self.grid_size = grid_size
        self.position = [0, 0]   # Starting position
at top-left
        self.q_table = {}   # Store state-action
values

    def get_state(self):
        return tuple(self.position)

    def choose_action(self):
        actions = ["up", "down", "left", "right"]
        return random.choice(actions)

    def take_action(self, action):
        if action == "up" and self.position[1] > 0:
```

```python
                self.position[1] -= 1
            elif action == "down" and self.position[1]
< self.grid_size - 1:
                self.position[1] += 1
            elif action == "left" and self.position[0]
> 0:
                self.position[0] -= 1
            elif action == "right" and self.position[0]
< self.grid_size - 1:
                self.position[0] += 1

    def learn(self, reward):
        state = self.get_state()
        self.q_table[state] = reward  # Simple
learning for demonstration
        print(f"{self.name} learned: {state} ->
Reward: {reward}")

# Simulating an RL agent
agent = RLAgent("Explorer", 5)
goal = [4, 4]

for _ in range(20):  # Simulating 20 actions
    current_state = agent.get_state()
    action = agent.choose_action()
    agent.take_action(action)
    if agent.get_state() == goal:
        agent.learn(10)  # Reward for reaching the
goal
        print(f"{agent.name} reached the goal!")
        break
    else:
        agent.learn(-1)  # Penalty for non-goal
states
```

In this example:

The agent explores a 5x5 grid.

It learns by associating states with rewards, improving its ability to reach the goal.

What is Adaptation in MAS?

Adaptation in MAS refers to an agent's ability to modify its behavior in response to environmental changes. While learning often focuses on improving performance over time, adaptation emphasizes real-time adjustments to unexpected conditions.

An adaptive agent must:

Detect changes in the environment.

Analyze the impact of these changes on its goals.

Adjust its strategies or actions accordingly.

Real-World Example of Adaptation

Consider a fleet of autonomous delivery drones. If one drone encounters bad weather, it must adapt by rerouting to a safer path. Simultaneously, it might communicate with nearby drones to redistribute its delivery tasks, ensuring minimal disruption to the overall system.

Code Example: Adaptive Agent

Here's an example of an agent that adapts to environmental changes:

class Adaptive Agent:

```
    def __init__(self, name):
        self.name = name
        self.energy = 100
        self.task = None

    def perceive_environment(self, environment):
        self.low_energy =
environment.get("low_energy", False)
        self.new_task = environment.get("new_task",
None)

    def adapt(self):
        if self.low_energy:
            self.recharge()
        elif self.new_task:
            self.assign_task(self.new_task)
```

```
        else:
            print(f"{self.name}: Continuing current
task.")

    def recharge(self):
        self.energy = 100
        print(f"{self.name}: Recharged energy to
{self.energy}.")

    def assign_task(self, task):
        self.task = task
        print(f"{self.name}: Assigned new task:
{task}")

# Simulating an adaptive agent
agent = AdaptiveAgent("Worker-1")
environment = {"low_energy": True, "new_task":
"Deliver package"}

agent.perceive_environment(environment)
agent.adapt()
```

In this example:

The agent perceives changes in its energy level and task assignments.

It adapts by recharging or switching to a new task as needed.

The true strength of MAS lies in combining learning and adaptation. An agent that learns over time and adapts in real time can handle both short-term challenges and long-term improvements. Let's explore a practical example where these concepts are combined.

Exercise: Learning and Adapting Together

In this exercise, the agent learns from rewards while adapting to environmental changes:

class LearningAdaptiveAgent:

```
    def __init__(self, name):
```

```python
        self.name = name
        self.q_table = {}
        self.energy = 100

    def perceive(self, environment):
        self.low_energy =
environment.get("low_energy", False)
        self.task = environment.get("task", "idle")

    def decide(self):
        if self.low_energy:
            return "recharge"
        elif self.task != "idle":
            return f"perform {self.task}"
        else:
            return "idle"

    def act(self, decision):
        if decision == "recharge":
            self.energy = 100
            print(f"{self.name}: Recharging
energy.")
        elif "perform" in decision:
            self.energy -= 10
            print(f"{self.name}: {decision}.
Energy: {self.energy}")
            self.learn(decision, 10)  # Reward for
completing tasks
        else:
            print(f"{self.name}: Idle.")

    def learn(self, task, reward):
        self.q_table[task] = reward
        print(f"{self.name} learned: {task} ->
Reward: {reward}")

# Simulate environment and agent
agent = LearningAdaptiveAgent("Agent-1")
environment_states = [
    {"low_energy": False, "task": "deliver
package"},
    {"low_energy": True, "task": "idle"},
```

```
    {"low_energy": False, "task": "pick item"},
]

for environment in environment_states:
    agent.perceive(environment)
    decision = agent.decide()
    agent.act(decision)
```

This example shows:

How an agent learns task rewards while adapting to its energy level.

How learning enhances long-term efficiency while adaptation ensures immediate functionality.

Applications of Learning and Adaptation in MAS

Autonomous Vehicles: Vehicles learn optimal routes over time while adapting to traffic and weather conditions.

Smart Grids: Energy management systems learn consumption patterns and adapt to fluctuating demand.

Robotics: Robots in manufacturing plants learn efficient workflows while adapting to equipment failures or changes in production.

Learning and adaptation are transformative capabilities in multi-agent systems. By equipping agents with the ability to learn from their experiences and adapt to real-time changes, you create systems that are not only intelligent but also resilient and responsive. The examples and exercises in this section provide practical insights into implementing these capabilities, empowering you to build MAS that thrive in dynamic, unpredictable environments.

Chapter 4: Revolutionizing Automation with Multi-Agent Systems

Multi-agent systems (MAS) are reshaping how automation is implemented across industries, offering solutions that are adaptive, scalable, and efficient. Unlike traditional centralized systems, MAS leverage the collective intelligence of independent agents to handle complex tasks collaboratively. In this chapter, we'll explore how MAS are transforming three key domains: **industry and manufacturing, autonomous vehicles and traffic systems**, and **healthcare**. By understanding these applications, you'll see the revolutionary potential of MAS in the modern world.

4.1 Applications in Industry and Manufacturing

The industrial and manufacturing sectors have always been at the forefront of adopting new technologies. Today, multi-agent systems (MAS) are revolutionizing these industries by making operations more adaptive, efficient, and resilient. Unlike traditional systems that rely on centralized control, MAS enable a decentralized approach where individual agents, such as robots, machines, and software components, collaborate to achieve shared goals. This section explores the diverse applications of MAS in industry and manufacturing, with practical examples, real-world insights, and detailed explanations to ensure you fully grasp their transformative potential.

The Role of MAS in Industry

At the heart of MAS in industry is the concept of autonomy and collaboration. Each agent—whether a robot on an assembly line or a software component managing inventory—operates independently while coordinating with other agents to optimize the entire system. This decentralization not only enhances efficiency but also allows the system to adapt in real time to changing conditions, such as equipment failures or fluctuations in demand.

Let's consider a car manufacturing plant. In traditional systems, a central controller assigns tasks to robots, monitors progress, and manages resources. While effective for predictable environments, this approach struggles in dynamic settings. MAS addresses this by allowing robots (agents) to make decisions locally. For instance, if a welding robot malfunctions, nearby robots can collaborate to take over its tasks without waiting for central instructions. This improves uptime and reduces bottlenecks.

Smart Factories: The Cornerstone of Industry 4.0

Smart factories are the epitome of MAS implementation in manufacturing. They integrate robots, sensors, and software agents into a cohesive ecosystem that optimizes production. Let's break this down with a real-world perspective:

Autonomous Robots:

In a smart factory, robots are agents capable of perceiving their surroundings, deciding on tasks, and acting accordingly. For example, an autonomous robot might transport materials between workstations, rerouting itself dynamically if it encounters obstacles.

Sensor Networks:

Sensors act as agents that monitor the environment, such as temperature, humidity, and equipment performance. They communicate this data to other agents, triggering actions like adjusting machine settings or scheduling maintenance.

Dynamic Scheduling:

Software agents manage production schedules by analyzing real-time data. If a delay occurs in one process, the schedule is adjusted dynamically to minimize downtime.

Dynamic Task Allocation

Dynamic task allocation is one of the most impactful applications of MAS in manufacturing. Instead of relying on pre-assigned roles, agents decide in real time who is best suited to handle specific tasks. This flexibility improves resource utilization and reduces idle time.

Here's a practical example:

Code Example: Dynamic Task Allocation

class Robot Agent:

```
    def __init__(self, name):
```

```python
        self.name = name
        self.available = True

    def assign_task(self, task):
        if self.available:
            print(f"{self.name} is assigned task:
{task}")
            self.available = False
        else:
            print(f"{self.name} is currently
busy.")

    def complete_task(self):
        self.available = True
        print(f"{self.name} has completed the task
and is now available.")

# Create robots
robots = [RobotAgent(f"Robot-{i}") for i in
range(3)]
tasks = ["Assemble part A", "Inspect part B",
"Transport materials"]

# Allocate tasks dynamically
for i, task in enumerate(tasks):
    robots[i % len(robots)].assign_task(task)
```

In this example:

Each robot checks its availability before taking on a task.

Tasks are distributed dynamically, ensuring optimal resource use.

Real-World Example: Amazon's Robotic Warehouses

Amazon's fulfillment centers are a prime example of MAS in action. Thousands of autonomous robots, known as **Kiva robots**, collaborate to optimize the picking and packing process. Each robot is an agent that:

Carries shelves of products to human workers for packing.

Communicates with other robots to avoid collisions.

Optimizes its route based on real-time traffic data within the warehouse.

This decentralized approach allows Amazon to handle millions of orders daily with unparalleled efficiency.

Predictive Maintenance with MAS

Another transformative application of MAS in manufacturing is predictive maintenance. In traditional systems, equipment is maintained on a fixed schedule, which can lead to unnecessary downtime or unexpected failures. MAS enable predictive maintenance by using agents to monitor equipment conditions and predict when maintenance is needed.

How It Works:

Sensors (agents) collect data on parameters like vibration, temperature, and pressure.

Software agents analyze this data to detect anomalies or signs of wear.

Maintenance agents schedule repairs proactively, reducing downtime and extending equipment lifespan.

Code Example: Predictive Maintenance

class Sensor Agent:

```
    def __init__(self, name):
        self.name = name

    def monitor(self, value):
        if value > 80:   # Threshold for anomaly
            return f"{self.name}: Alert! Value
{value} exceeds threshold."
        return f"{self.name}: Value {value} is
normal."

# Create sensor agents
sensor1 = SensorAgent("TemperatureSensor")
sensor2 = SensorAgent("VibrationSensor")

# Simulate monitoring
print(sensor1.monitor(85))   # Exceeds threshold
print(sensor2.monitor(60))   # Normal value
```

This example demonstrates how agents monitor equipment and raise alerts when anomalies are detected.

Collaborative Robotics in Assembly Lines

Collaborative robots, or cobots, are designed to work alongside humans. MAS enable these robots to adapt their behavior based on human actions, ensuring safety and efficiency.

For example, in an electronics assembly line:

A cobot places components on a circuit board.

It monitors the speed of its human coworker and adjusts its pace to match.

If a human signals for help, the cobot provides assistance, such as holding parts in place.

This seamless interaction is made possible by MAS principles, where each cobot operates autonomously but collaborates effectively with its environment and peers.

Real-World Example: BMW's Adaptive Assembly Lines

BMW uses MAS to create adaptive assembly lines where robots and humans work together. Robots perform repetitive tasks like screwing and welding, while humans handle complex assembly processes. The robots adjust their behavior based on human actions, ensuring smooth collaboration.

Challenges in MAS Implementation

While MAS offer significant benefits, they also come with challenges:

Inter-Agent Communication: Ensuring agents understand each other, especially when developed by different teams.

Scalability: Managing communication and coordination as the number of agents grows.

Security: Protecting MAS from cyberattacks, particularly in critical systems.

The application of MAS in industry and manufacturing is transforming these sectors, making them more adaptive, efficient, and resilient. From dynamic task allocation to predictive maintenance and collaborative robotics, MAS are enabling smart factories that can handle the complexities of modern production. As technology advances, the integration of MAS with AI, IoT, and machine learning will further enhance their capabilities, paving the way for the next wave of industrial innovation. The practical examples and insights shared here provide a strong foundation for understanding how MAS can revolutionize manufacturing.

4.2 Autonomous Vehicles and Traffic Systems

Autonomous vehicles (AVs) and intelligent traffic systems represent some of the most groundbreaking applications of multi-agent systems (MAS). By enabling vehicles, infrastructure, and traffic management systems to work together as independent yet cooperative agents, MAS transforms the way we manage transportation. These systems address real-world challenges like traffic congestion, road safety, and fuel efficiency, delivering solutions that are both adaptive and scalable.

The Role of MAS in Autonomous Vehicles

An autonomous vehicle is more than just a self-driving car—it's a sophisticated agent operating in a dynamic environment. MAS enhances AVs by enabling collaboration among vehicles, infrastructure, and traffic systems, allowing them to:

Communicate in real time.

Coordinate actions like lane changes and intersections.

Adapt to changing road conditions.

For instance, a single autonomous car can navigate a road, but when multiple AVs communicate and coordinate, the entire traffic system becomes smoother and safer. Imagine one vehicle informing others about a sudden slowdown, allowing them to adjust their speeds preemptively.

Core Functions of Autonomous Vehicle Agents

Perception:
 AVs perceive their surroundings using sensors like cameras, radar, and LiDAR. This perception helps them identify obstacles, lanes, and other vehicles.

Decision-Making:
 Based on their perception, AVs decide on actions like braking, accelerating, or changing lanes.

Communication:
 AVs share information with other agents—such as nearby vehicles, traffic lights, or cloud systems—facilitating coordination.

Adaptation:
 AVs adapt to unexpected changes like roadblocks, weather conditions, or accidents, ensuring continuous functionality.

Vehicle-to-Vehicle (V2V) Communication

In MAS-driven traffic systems, V2V communication enables vehicles to share real-time data. For example:

If a car encounters a slippery road, it alerts nearby vehicles, helping them adjust their driving behavior.

During a lane change, one vehicle informs others to ensure a smooth transition without collisions.

Practical Code Example: V2V Communication

Here's a simple simulation of two vehicles communicating about lane changes:

class Vehicle Agent:

```
    def __init__(self, name, position):
        self.name = name
        self.position = position

    def send_message(self, recipient, message):
        print(f"{self.name} to {recipient.name}: 
{message}")
        recipient.receive_message(self, message)
```

```
    def receive_message(self, sender, message):
        print(f"{self.name} received from
{sender.name}: {message}")

# Create two vehicles
vehicle1 = VehicleAgent("Car-1", 10)
vehicle2 = VehicleAgent("Car-2", 12)

# Simulate lane change communication
vehicle1.send_message(vehicle2, "Requesting
permission to change lanes.")
vehicle2.receive_message(vehicle1, "Requesting
permission to change lanes.")
vehicle2.send_message(vehicle1, "Permission
granted. Safe to change lanes.")
```

This example demonstrates how vehicles can communicate to coordinate actions like lane changes, ensuring safety and efficiency.

MAS in Traffic Systems

Traffic systems powered by MAS go beyond managing individual vehicles. They treat traffic lights, intersections, and road sensors as agents, enabling them to work together to optimize traffic flow.

Traffic Light Optimization

Traditional traffic lights operate on fixed timers, often leading to inefficiencies during fluctuating traffic conditions. MAS-based traffic lights, however, adapt dynamically by communicating with nearby lights and vehicles.

How It Works:

Sensors detect vehicle density at an intersection.

Traffic lights adjust their durations based on real-time data.

Nearby lights coordinate to prevent bottlenecks.

Real-World Example: Smart Traffic Systems in Los Angeles

Los Angeles implemented an intelligent traffic system where MAS principles guide over 4,500 traffic signals. The system reduces congestion by adjusting light timings dynamically, based on real-time traffic conditions.

Vehicle Platooning

Platooning refers to a group of vehicles traveling closely together, maintaining synchronization to reduce air resistance and fuel consumption. In a MAS, each vehicle in the platoon acts as an agent, coordinating with others to maintain safe distances and speeds.

Code Example: Vehicle Platooning

Here's a basic simulation of platooning behavior:

class PlatoonVehicle:

```
    def __init__(self, name, speed):
        self.name = name
        self.speed = speed

    def synchronize_speed(self, leader_speed):
        self.speed = leader_speed
        print(f"{self.name}: Adjusted speed to
{self.speed} km/h to match the platoon leader.")

# Simulate a platoon of vehicles
leader = PlatoonVehicle("Leader", 80)
follower1 = PlatoonVehicle("Follower-1", 70)
follower2 = PlatoonVehicle("Follower-2", 75)

# Synchronize speeds
follower1.synchronize_speed(leader.speed)
follower2.synchronize_speed(leader.speed)
```

This example shows how vehicles in a platoon adjust their speeds to maintain synchronization.

Adaptation in Traffic Systems

MAS-based traffic systems adapt to disruptions like accidents, road closures, or weather changes. For example, if an accident occurs on a busy highway:

Sensors detect the congestion.

Traffic lights along alternate routes adjust to redirect vehicles.

Digital signage provides real-time updates to drivers.

Real-World Example: Singapore's Traffic Management System

Singapore's MAS-driven traffic system uses sensors and cameras to monitor road conditions. The system adapts dynamically by redirecting traffic and adjusting light timings to minimize delays.

Challenges in MAS-Driven Traffic Systems

While MAS offers immense benefits, implementing it in traffic systems comes with challenges:

Scalability: Managing communication among thousands of vehicles and infrastructure agents can be complex.

Security: V2V communication must be secure to prevent hacking or tampering.

Interoperability: Ensuring compatibility between different vehicle manufacturers and systems is critical.

The application of MAS in autonomous vehicles and traffic systems is transforming transportation, making it safer, more efficient, and more sustainable. From V2V communication to intelligent traffic lights and vehicle platooning, MAS creates a collaborative ecosystem where agents work together seamlessly. The examples and insights provided here illustrate how MAS addresses real-world challenges, paving the way for a future of smarter, more connected transportation. By leveraging MAS principles, we can reimagine how we move, reducing congestion and environmental impact while improving overall mobility.

4.3 Transforming Healthcare with Multi-Agent Systems

Healthcare is one of the most complex systems we interact with daily. It involves a wide range of interconnected components—patients, doctors, medical devices, hospital systems, and more. Multi-agent systems (MAS) are transforming this landscape by introducing automation, adaptability, and efficiency. By enabling independent agents to collaborate, MAS helps optimize healthcare delivery, reduce operational inefficiencies, and provide personalized care.

How MAS Enhances Healthcare

The complexity of healthcare makes it a perfect fit for MAS. Each agent in the system, whether physical (e.g., medical devices) or virtual (e.g., software), can work independently to achieve specific goals while collaborating with other agents. This creates a decentralized system that can respond to real-time challenges, such as managing hospital resources during emergencies or ensuring continuity of care for chronic disease patients.

Hospital Resource Management

Managing resources like operating rooms, hospital beds, and staff availability is a critical challenge in healthcare. MAS simplifies this by representing each resource as an agent capable of communicating with others to allocate tasks efficiently.

Scenario: Scheduling Surgeries

Imagine a hospital where operating rooms (ORs) are constantly in demand. Each OR acts as an agent, coordinating with surgeon agents and patient agents to optimize schedules. If one OR becomes unavailable due to maintenance, other ORs adapt their schedules to accommodate the affected cases.

Code Example: Resource Allocation

Here's a simplified implementation of MAS for scheduling surgeries:

class Resource Agent:

```
def __init__(self, name, available=True):
    self.name = name
    self.available = available

def assign_task(self, task):
    if self.available:
        self.available = False
```

```
            print(f"{self.name} is assigned task:
{task}")
        else:
            print(f"{self.name} is unavailable.")

    def complete_task(self):
        self.available = True
        print(f"{self.name} has completed the task
and is now available.")

# Create resources (operating rooms)
or1 = ResourceAgent("OperatingRoom-1")
or2 = ResourceAgent("OperatingRoom-2")

# Assign tasks (surgeries)
or1.assign_task("Surgery A")
or2.assign_task("Surgery B")

# Complete tasks
or1.complete_task()
or1.assign_task("Surgery C")
```

This example shows how agents can represent resources like operating rooms, dynamically allocating tasks based on availability.

Real-Time Monitoring and Alerts

In modern healthcare, wearable devices and sensors play a crucial role in monitoring patient health. Each device acts as an agent, collecting data like heart rate, oxygen levels, or glucose levels. These agents communicate with healthcare systems to provide real-time alerts, ensuring timely intervention.

Scenario: Monitoring Chronic Disease Patients

Consider a diabetic patient wearing a continuous glucose monitor. The device (agent) tracks glucose levels and communicates with a smartphone app (another agent). If glucose levels drop too low, the system sends an alert to the patient and their doctor, enabling prompt action.

Code Example: Real-Time Monitoring

class Monitoring Device:

```
def __init__(self, name):
    self.name = name

def monitor(self, value):
    if value < 70:   # Low glucose level
threshold
        return f"{self.name}: Alert! Glucose
level {value} is too low."
    elif value > 180:   # High glucose level
threshold
        return f"{self.name}: Alert! Glucose
level {value} is too high."
    else:
        return f"{self.name}: Glucose level
{value} is normal."

# Simulate glucose monitoring
device = MonitoringDevice("GlucoseMonitor")
print(device.monitor(65))   # Low glucose
print(device.monitor(120))   # Normal glucose
```

This example illustrates how monitoring devices can provide real-time alerts based on patient data.

Personalized Medicine

Personalized medicine tailors treatments to individual patients based on their genetic, clinical, and lifestyle data. MAS enhances this process by enabling agents to collaborate and analyze different data sources, providing precise recommendations.

Scenario: Recommending Cancer Treatments

In oncology, treatment plans often depend on genetic mutations, tumor characteristics, and patient health. MAS can represent each data source (e.g., genetic test results, imaging data) as an agent. These agents collaborate to recommend targeted therapies, improving treatment outcomes.

Code Example: Treatment Recommendation

class Patient Agent:

```python
    def __init__(self, name, genetic_data,
symptoms):
        self.name = name
        self.genetic_data = genetic_data
        self.symptoms = symptoms

    def recommend_treatment(self):
        if "mutation-X" in self.genetic_data:
            return "Administer targeted therapy for
mutation-X"
        elif "fever" in self.symptoms:
            return "Prescribe antipyretic"
        else:
            return "Perform further diagnosis"

# Simulate personalized treatment recommendation
patient = PatientAgent("Patient-1", ["mutation-X"],
["fever"])
print(f"{patient.name}: Recommended treatment -
{patient.recommend_treatment()}")
```

This example shows how agents can analyze patient data to provide personalized treatment recommendations.

Emergency Response Systems

During emergencies like natural disasters or pandemics, MAS can coordinate resources, triage patients, and optimize care delivery. Each agent represents a critical component, such as ambulances, hospital beds, or medical supplies, working together to ensure timely responses.

Scenario: Ambulance Coordination

In an emergency, MAS can allocate ambulances dynamically, ensuring the closest available unit responds to a patient while other agents update hospital availability.

Real-World Example: IBM Watson Health

IBM Watson Health demonstrates MAS in action by analyzing patient data, medical records, and research papers to assist doctors in diagnosing diseases and recommending treatments. Each module of Watson acts as an agent specializing in a specific task, like identifying symptoms or suggesting medications. This collaborative approach improves accuracy and reduces the time needed for decision-making.

Challenges in MAS Implementation in Healthcare

While MAS offers transformative potential, implementing it in healthcare comes with challenges:

Data Privacy: Ensuring patient data is secure and compliant with regulations like HIPAA.

Interoperability: Integrating agents from different systems and manufacturers seamlessly.

Scalability: Managing communication and coordination in large healthcare networks.

Multi-agent systems are transforming healthcare by making it more efficient, personalized, and responsive. From optimizing hospital resources to enabling real-time monitoring and tailoring treatments, MAS addresses critical challenges in the healthcare ecosystem. The practical examples and real-world applications shared here illustrate how MAS can enhance patient outcomes and operational efficiency. As technology evolves, MAS will play an even greater role in shaping the future of healthcare, ensuring better care for all.

Chapter 5: Enabling Collaboration Through Multi-Agent Systems

Collaboration lies at the heart of multi-agent systems (MAS). By enabling both **human-agent collaboration** and **inter-agent cooperation**, MAS fosters systems that are not only efficient but also highly adaptive to complex and dynamic challenges. These collaborative systems allow humans and agents to work together seamlessly, while agents themselves coordinate and solve problems collectively. In this chapter, we'll explore how collaboration is enabled in MAS, using detailed explanations, practical examples, and real-world case studies to illustrate the concepts.

5.1 Human-Agent Collaboration

Human-agent collaboration is one of the most transformative aspects of multi-agent systems (MAS). It involves creating systems where humans and agents work together seamlessly, leveraging the strengths of each to achieve goals more efficiently than either could independently. This collaboration spans across industries—healthcare, manufacturing, customer service, and more—offering solutions that are not only innovative but also deeply impactful.

Human-agent collaboration refers to the interaction between humans and intelligent agents to achieve shared objectives. Agents act as autonomous or semi-autonomous assistants, augmenting human capabilities by handling repetitive tasks, providing insights, or executing decisions based on predefined parameters.

For instance:

In healthcare, agents can assist doctors by analyzing medical data to suggest diagnoses.

In customer service, chatbots can handle common queries, freeing human agents to focus on complex issues.

In factories, collaborative robots (cobots) work alongside humans, performing repetitive or physically demanding tasks.

Key Principles of Human-Agent Collaboration

1. Complementary Strengths

Humans excel at creativity, intuition, and ethical decision-making, while agents are better at handling large volumes of data, repetitive tasks, and computationally intensive operations. Effective collaboration leverages these complementary strengths.

For example, in finance, an agent might analyze market data to identify trends, while a human trader interprets those trends within a broader economic context.

2. Transparency and Explainability

Humans need to trust agents, especially in high-stakes domains like healthcare or finance. Transparency is achieved when agents explain their reasoning and actions clearly, enabling humans to validate decisions and intervene if necessary.

Here's a simple Python example of an agent providing explainable recommendations:

class Medical Agent:

```python
    def __init__(self, name):
        self.name = name

    def recommend_treatment(self, symptoms):
        if "fever" in symptoms:
            return "Prescribe antipyretic", "Fever
detected; reduces body temperature."
        elif "cough" in symptoms:
            return "Prescribe cough suppressant",
"Cough detected; soothes throat irritation."
        else:
            return "Perform further diagnosis",
"Symptoms unclear; additional data required."

# Human-Agent Interaction
agent = MedicalAgent("HealthAssistant")
symptoms = ["fever", "headache"]
recommendation, explanation =
agent.recommend_treatment(symptoms)
print(f"Agent Recommendation: {recommendation}")
```

```
print(f"Explanation: {explanation}")
```

In this example:

The agent not only provides a recommendation but also explains its reasoning.

The human can evaluate the explanation before proceeding.

3. Adaptability

Agents should adapt to human preferences, behavior, and feedback. For instance, a smart home assistant might learn your daily routine, adjusting lights and temperature based on your habits.

Applications of Human-Agent Collaboration

1. Healthcare

In healthcare, agents assist doctors, nurses, and patients by providing diagnostic insights, automating administrative tasks, and monitoring patient health.

Example: Telemedicine

A telemedicine system might include an agent that collects patient symptoms, analyzes them, and prepares a summary for the doctor. The doctor reviews the summary and makes the final diagnosis.

2. Manufacturing

In factories, collaborative robots (cobots) work side by side with humans. These robots handle repetitive or heavy tasks, while humans focus on assembly, quality control, or problem-solving.

Real-World Example: Automotive Assembly

In automotive assembly lines, cobots install screws or weld parts while humans install complex components like electrical systems. Cobots adjust their speed and force to avoid accidents, ensuring safe collaboration.

3. Customer Service

Chatbots are a common example of human-agent collaboration in customer service. Agents handle routine queries, while human representatives take over complex cases.

Code Example: Chatbot Assistant

Here's a chatbot that assists a customer service agent by handling simple queries:

class Chatbot Agent:

```
    def __init__(self, name):
        self.name = name

    def handle_query(self, query):
        if query == "What are your business
hours?":
            return "We are open from 9 AM to 5 PM,
Monday to Friday."
        elif query == "Where is your location?":
            return "Our office is at 123 Main
Street, Springfield."
        else:
            return "Let me connect you to a human
representative."

# Simulate chatbot interaction
chatbot = ChatbotAgent("HelpBot")
customer_query = "What are your business hours?"
response = chatbot.handle_query(customer_query)
print(f"Chatbot Response: {response}")
```

In this example:

The chatbot provides quick answers to common questions.

For complex queries, it redirects to a human representative, ensuring efficient collaboration.

Designing Effective Human-Agent Collaboration Systems

Designing systems where humans and agents collaborate effectively requires careful consideration of several factors:

User Interface: The interface should be intuitive, allowing humans to interact with agents effortlessly.

Feedback Loops: Humans should provide feedback to agents, enabling continuous improvement.

Error Handling: The system must allow humans to intervene when agents encounter errors or uncertainties.

Exercise: Adaptive Task Assignment

Here's an exercise to simulate adaptive collaboration between a human and an agent:

class Assistant Agent:

```
def __init__(self, name):
    self.name = name

def suggest_task(self, workload):
    if workload < 5:
        return "You can handle this task."
    else:
        return "I'll take care of this task for
you."

# Simulate collaboration
agent = AssistantAgent("TaskHelper")
human_workload = 6
suggestion = agent.suggest_task(human_workload)
print(f"Agent Suggestion: {suggestion}")
```

This example demonstrates how agents adapt based on the human's workload, ensuring balanced task distribution.

Challenges in Human-Agent Collaboration

Trust: Humans may hesitate to rely on agents, especially in critical tasks.

Bias: Agents trained on biased data may make unfair or incorrect decisions.

Over-Reliance: Over-reliance on agents can lead to skill degradation among humans.

Human-agent collaboration is transforming how we work, live, and solve problems. By complementing human strengths with the efficiency and precision of agents, MAS creates systems that are both innovative and practical. From healthcare and manufacturing to customer service, the applications of this collaboration are vast and growing. Through transparency, adaptability, and assistive design, these systems enhance productivity and improve outcomes, offering a glimpse into the future of intelligent collaboration.

5.2 Inter-Agent Cooperation and Problem Solving

In a multi-agent system (MAS), agents don't work in isolation. Instead, they collaborate and cooperate to solve complex problems that would be too difficult or inefficient for a single agent to handle alone. Inter-agent cooperation is one of the core strengths of MAS, allowing agents to share knowledge, divide tasks, and align their goals effectively.

Inter-agent cooperation is the process by which agents work together to achieve shared objectives. Cooperation can involve:

Sharing information to create a collective understanding of the problem.

Dividing tasks based on the capabilities and availability of each agent.

Resolving conflicts and negotiating solutions when goals or resource needs overlap.

For example, in a rescue mission involving drones, each drone might survey a different area, share findings with others, and coordinate their movements to avoid duplication or collisions. This kind of cooperation ensures that the mission is completed faster and more efficiently.

Mechanisms of Cooperation

For agents to cooperate effectively, they rely on specific mechanisms:

1. Communication

Agents communicate with each other to share information, such as status updates, task progress, or environmental observations. This can be done through direct messaging, broadcasts, or shared data repositories.

2. Task Allocation

In cooperative systems, agents decide who will handle which tasks. This can be based on factors like proximity, expertise, or current workload.

3. Negotiation

When agents have conflicting goals or need to share limited resources, they negotiate to find mutually acceptable solutions.

4. Shared Goals

Agents align their individual objectives with the overall goals of the system, ensuring that their actions contribute to the collective success.

Practical Example: Coordinating Warehouse Robots

Let's consider a warehouse where multiple robots collaborate to fulfill orders. Each robot is an agent capable of picking items, transporting them, and updating the system with its status.

Code Example: Task Allocation in a Warehouse

class Robot Agent:

```
def __init__(self, name, capacity):
    self.name = name
    self.capacity = capacity
    self.current_load = 0
    self.tasks = []

def assign_task(self, task):
    if self.current_load < self.capacity:
        self.tasks.append(task)
        self.current_load += 1
        print(f"{self.name} assigned task: {task}")
    else:
        print(f"{self.name} is at full capacity. Task {task} cannot be assigned.")

def share_status(self):
```

```
        print(f"{self.name}: Current load -
{self.current_load}/{self.capacity}, Tasks -
{self.tasks}")

# Create robots
robot1 = RobotAgent("Robot-1", 2)
robot2 = RobotAgent("Robot-2", 3)

# Assign tasks
tasks = ["Pick Item A", "Pick Item B", "Transport
Item C", "Deliver Item D"]
for i, task in enumerate(tasks):
    if i % 2 == 0:
        robot1.assign_task(task)
    else:
        robot2.assign_task(task)

# Share status
robot1.share_status()
robot2.share_status()
```

In this example:

Each robot agent has a capacity that limits how many tasks it can handle simultaneously.

Tasks are distributed dynamically, ensuring optimal use of resources.

Real-World Applications of Cooperative MAS

1. Autonomous Vehicles in Traffic Systems

In intelligent traffic systems, autonomous vehicles communicate and coordinate with each other to optimize traffic flow. For example:

Vehicles approaching an intersection negotiate right-of-way to avoid collisions.

Cars traveling in a convoy adjust their speeds to maintain a safe distance while reducing fuel consumption.

Practical Code Example: Vehicle Coordination

class Vehicle Agent:

```
    def __init__(self, name, position):
        self.name = name
        self.position = position

    def negotiate_position(self, other_vehicle):
        if abs(self.position -
other_vehicle.position) < 10:
            print(f"{self.name}: Adjusting speed to
avoid collision with {other_vehicle.name}.")
        else:
            print(f"{self.name}: Safe distance from
{other_vehicle.name}.")

# Create vehicles
vehicle1 = VehicleAgent("Car-1", 50)
vehicle2 = VehicleAgent("Car-2", 55)

# Simulate negotiation
vehicle1.negotiate_position(vehicle2)
vehicle2.negotiate_position(vehicle1)
```

This demonstrates how agents cooperate to maintain safety in dynamic environments.

2. Disaster Response and Rescue Operations

In disaster scenarios, MAS enables drones, robots, and sensors to collaborate:

Drones survey affected areas, sharing images and data.

Robots perform search-and-rescue operations based on data from drones.

Sensors detect survivors and guide rescue agents to their locations.

3. Energy Management in Smart Grids

In smart grids, energy producers, storage units, and consumers act as agents. They coordinate to balance supply and demand, ensuring efficient energy distribution.

Cooperative Problem-Solving Techniques

Cooperation often requires agents to solve problems collectively. Here are some common approaches:

Distributed Problem Solving

Agents work on different parts of the problem independently and then combine their results to form a complete solution.

Consensus Algorithms

Agents reach agreement on shared decisions, such as resource allocation or scheduling.

Exercise: Distributed Task Execution

Here's an exercise where agents share a complex task and execute it cooperatively:

class Worker Agent:

```python
    def __init__(self, name):
        self.name = name
        self.task = None

    def assign_subtask(self, subtask):
        self.task = subtask
        print(f"{self.name} assigned subtask:
{subtask}")

    def complete_task(self):
        print(f"{self.name} completed subtask:
{self.task}")
        self.task = None

# Create agents
worker1 = WorkerAgent("Worker-1")
worker2 = WorkerAgent("Worker-2")

# Divide a task into subtasks
subtasks = ["Analyze Data", "Generate Report"]

# Assign subtasks
worker1.assign_subtask(subtasks[0])
worker2.assign_subtask(subtasks[1])
```

```
# Complete tasks
worker1.complete_task()
worker2.complete_task()
```

This exercise illustrates how agents divide and complete a task collaboratively.

Challenges in Inter-Agent Cooperation

Conflict Resolution: Agents may have conflicting goals, requiring negotiation to find a balance.

Communication Overhead: Excessive communication can slow down the system, especially in large-scale MAS.

Trust: Agents must rely on the accuracy and honesty of shared information.

Inter-agent cooperation and problem solving are fundamental to the success of multi-agent systems. By enabling agents to share information, align their goals, and divide tasks dynamically, MAS tackles complex problems efficiently. From coordinating robots in warehouses to managing autonomous vehicles in traffic systems, the applications of cooperative MAS are vast and impactful. The examples and exercises provided here demonstrate the practical aspects of building cooperative systems, equipping you with the tools to create MAS that excel in collaboration.

5.3 Case Studies in Collaborative MAS

Multi-agent systems (MAS) thrive in environments where collaboration is essential. By enabling agents to cooperate, adapt, and solve problems collectively, MAS can address complex challenges in a way no centralized system could. This section presents real-world case studies where collaborative MAS have been implemented successfully, offering detailed insights into their architecture, operation, and impact.

Case Study 1: Smart Traffic Management in Singapore

Overview

Traffic congestion is a major problem in urban areas, leading to wasted time, increased pollution, and economic losses. Singapore's smart traffic management system employs MAS to optimize traffic flow, reduce congestion, and improve safety. The system treats traffic lights, vehicles, and road sensors as agents, allowing them to communicate and coordinate dynamically.

How It Works

Agents Involved:

Traffic Lights: These agents adapt their timings based on vehicle density and pedestrian activity.

Vehicles: Autonomous vehicles (AVs) act as agents, communicating with each other and with traffic lights to anticipate signal changes and adjust their speed.

Road Sensors: Sensors monitor traffic density and send real-time data to traffic lights and central systems.

Cooperation Mechanism:
Traffic lights negotiate green light durations based on traffic flow in adjacent areas.

Vehicles share speed and position data to coordinate lane changes and avoid congestion.

Sensors provide traffic density updates to ensure timely adjustments.

Practical Example: Traffic Light Coordination

Below is a simplified Python example that demonstrates how traffic lights coordinate:

class TrafficLightAgent:

```
def __init__(self, name, traffic_density):
    self.name = name
    self.traffic_density = traffic_density

def adjust_timing(self, neighbor):
```

```
        if self.traffic_density >
neighbor.traffic_density:
            print(f"{self.name} extends green light
duration.")
        else:
            print(f"{self.name} reduces green light
duration.")

# Create traffic light agents
light1 = TrafficLightAgent("Light-1", 30)
light2 = TrafficLightAgent("Light-2", 20)

# Coordinate traffic light timings
light1.adjust_timing(light2)
light2.adjust_timing(light1)
```

This example shows how agents compare traffic densities to adjust their timings, ensuring smoother traffic flow.

Impact

Singapore's MAS-driven traffic system has:

Reduced average commute times by 12%.

Lowered vehicle emissions by optimizing stop-and-go patterns.

Improved pedestrian safety with adaptive signal timing.

Case Study 2: Collaborative Robotics in Amazon Warehouses

Overview

Amazon's fulfillment centers handle millions of orders daily, requiring efficient coordination of robots, workers, and inventory. To achieve this, Amazon employs MAS where robots act as agents that autonomously navigate warehouses, retrieve items, and deliver them to human packers.

How It Works

Agents Involved:

Robots: Each robot acts as an agent with the ability to navigate, detect obstacles, and optimize its path.

Inventory Systems: These systems track the location of products and communicate with robots to assign tasks.

Humans: Human packers interact with robots, focusing on tasks that require dexterity or decision-making.

Cooperation Mechanism:

Robots share their locations and paths to avoid collisions.

Inventory systems allocate tasks to robots based on proximity and workload.

Robots prioritize tasks dynamically, ensuring that high-priority orders are fulfilled first.

Practical Example: Task Coordination

Here's a Python simulation of robots coordinating tasks in a warehouse:

class Robot Agent:

```python
    def __init__(self, name, location):
        self.name = name
        self.location = location

    def assign_task(self, task,
inventory_location):
        print(f"{self.name} assigned task: {task}.
Moving to {inventory_location}.")
        self.location = inventory_location

    def avoid_collision(self, other_robot):
        if self.location == other_robot.location:
            print(f"{self.name} adjusts path to
avoid collision with {other_robot.name}.")
        else:
            print(f"{self.name} and
{other_robot.name} are on safe paths.")

# Create robots
robot1 = RobotAgent("Robot-1", "A1")
robot2 = RobotAgent("Robot-2", "B1")

# Assign tasks and coordinate paths
```

```
robot1.assign_task("Pick Item X", "B1")
robot2.assign_task("Pick Item Y", "C1")
robot1.avoid_collision(robot2)
```

This example highlights how robots communicate to coordinate tasks and avoid collisions in real time.

Impact

Amazon's MAS implementation has resulted in:

A 25% increase in warehouse efficiency.

Reduced operational costs by automating repetitive tasks.

Enhanced safety with robots and humans working in harmony.

Case Study 3: Disaster Response with Collaborative Drones

Overview

In disaster scenarios, rapid assessment and resource allocation are critical. Collaborative MAS using drones have been deployed in disaster response missions to map affected areas, locate survivors, and deliver emergency supplies.

How It Works

Agents Involved:

Survey Drones: These drones map the area and identify obstacles.

Rescue Drones: They locate survivors using thermal imaging and relay coordinates to rescue teams.

Supply Drones: These deliver food, water, and medical supplies to survivors.

Cooperation Mechanism:

Survey drones share real-time maps with rescue and supply drones.

Rescue drones prioritize survivors based on urgency, coordinating with supply drones for delivery.

Drones negotiate paths to avoid collisions and optimize coverage.

Practical Example: Drone Cooperation

Below is a simulation of drones sharing tasks in a disaster zone:

class Drone Agent:

```
    def __init__(self, name, task):
        self.name = name
        self.task = task

    def share_task(self, other_drone):
        print(f"{self.name} sharing task with
{other_drone.name}: {self.task}")

# Create drones
drone1 = DroneAgent("SurveyDrone", "Map Area A")
drone2 = DroneAgent("RescueDrone", "Locate
Survivors in Area A")

# Coordinate tasks
drone1.share_task(drone2)
```

This example demonstrates how drones coordinate by sharing tasks to achieve their goals efficiently.

Impact

Collaborative drones have:

Reduced the time required to map disaster zones by 40%.

Improved survivor recovery rates by enabling faster resource delivery.

Enhanced safety for human responders by providing detailed situational awareness.

These case studies illustrate the transformative power of collaborative MAS in addressing real-world challenges. Whether optimizing traffic systems, streamlining warehouse operations, or responding to disasters, MAS enables agents to cooperate effectively, delivering results that surpass traditional methods.

Chapter 6: Challenges in Multi-Agent System Design

Designing multi-agent systems (MAS) brings immense possibilities, but it also comes with significant challenges. As systems grow in complexity, managing scalability, ethical considerations, and security becomes crucial. In this chapter, we will explore the primary challenges in MAS design, breaking them down into three core areas: managing scalability and complexity, addressing ethical considerations, and ensuring security and privacy. Through detailed explanations and real-world examples, we'll examine these challenges and how they can be addressed effectively.

6.1 Managing Scalability and Complexity

Scaling a multi-agent system (MAS) while maintaining its functionality is one of the most intricate challenges in MAS design. As the number of agents increases, the complexity of communication, coordination, and resource management grows exponentially. Systems that work well with a few agents can become unwieldy or inefficient when scaled to hundreds or thousands.

The Challenges of Scalability in MAS

Scalability is about ensuring that an MAS performs effectively as the number of agents or tasks grows. A scalable system maintains its efficiency without a significant drop in performance or reliability, even as the system expands. Here's why this is challenging:

1. Communication Overhead

As the number of agents increases, the amount of data exchanged grows exponentially. Each agent needs to communicate with others, leading to network congestion or delays.

Example:

Imagine a smart traffic system where every traffic light communicates with all others. In a small city, this might be manageable. However, in a large metropolitan area, the network could become overwhelmed with messages, causing delays or failures.

2. Coordination Complexity

With more agents, coordinating tasks and ensuring that agents don't duplicate efforts or interfere with each other becomes harder. Coordination must remain efficient even as agents join or leave the system dynamically.

Example:

In a warehouse, robots must coordinate to avoid collisions and optimize task completion. Adding more robots increases the risk of bottlenecks and task overlaps if coordination mechanisms aren't robust.

3. Resource Contention

When agents share resources like bandwidth, energy, or computational power, competition can lead to inefficiencies or deadlocks. This is especially critical in distributed systems.

Example:

In a smart grid, multiple energy storage agents may compete for limited power during peak demand, leading to resource conflicts.

Techniques for Managing Scalability

To address these challenges, MAS employs several strategies:

1. Hierarchical Architectures

In a hierarchical architecture, agents are grouped into levels. High-level agents handle global tasks like coordination, while low-level agents focus on local actions. This reduces the communication load, as not every agent needs to interact with all others.

Real-World Example:

In a smart city, district-level traffic controllers (high-level agents) coordinate intersections (low-level agents) within their area, ensuring efficient flow without city-wide communication.

Code Example: Hierarchical Coordination

class HighLevelAgent:

```
    def __init__(self, name):
```

```
        self.name = name

    def coordinate(self, low_level_agents):
        for agent in low_level_agents:
            print(f"{self.name}: Assigning task to
{agent.name}")

class LowLevelAgent:
    def __init__(self, name):
        self.name = name

    def perform_task(self, task):
        print(f"{self.name}: Performing {task}")

# Create agents
high_level_agent = HighLevelAgent("Controller-1")
low_level_agents = [LowLevelAgent(f"Intersection-
{i}") for i in range(3)]

# Coordinate tasks
high_level_agent.coordinate(low_level_agents)
for agent in low_level_agents:
    agent.perform_task("Optimize Traffic Flow")
```

Here, a high-level agent assigns tasks to low-level agents, reducing the need for direct communication between all agents.

2. Decentralized Decision-Making

Instead of relying on a central controller, decentralized systems allow agents to make decisions locally based on their environment and shared rules. This reduces the communication burden and ensures the system remains resilient.

Example:

In a fleet of delivery drones, each drone independently plans its route based on package destinations and traffic conditions, rather than waiting for centralized instructions.

Code Example: Decentralized Decision-Making

class Drone Agent:

```python
    def __init__(self, name, destination):
        self.name = name
        self.destination = destination

    def decide_route(self, weather, traffic):
        if weather == "clear" and traffic == "low":
            return f"{self.name}: Taking fastest
route to {self.destination}."
        else:
            return f"{self.name}: Adjusting route
to avoid delays."

# Simulate drones
drones = [
    DroneAgent("Drone-1", "Zone A"),
    DroneAgent("Drone-2", "Zone B"),
]

# Simulate environment
weather = "clear"
traffic = "high"

# Drones decide routes
for drone in drones:
    print(drone.decide_route(weather, traffic))
```

This example illustrates how agents make decisions based on local information, reducing the need for central coordination.

3. Task Decomposition

Breaking complex tasks into smaller subtasks allows agents to handle them independently. This distributes the workload and ensures scalability.

Example:

In disaster response, one drone surveys an area, another locates survivors, and a third delivers supplies. Each agent focuses on a specific subtask, ensuring efficiency.

Code Example: Task Decomposition

class Task Agent:

```python
    def __init__(self, name):
        self.name = name

    def execute_subtask(self, subtask):
        print(f"{self.name}: Executing {subtask}")

# Define subtasks
subtasks = ["Survey Area", "Locate Survivors",
"Deliver Supplies"]

# Assign subtasks to agents
agents = [TaskAgent(f"Drone-{i+1}") for i in
range(len(subtasks))]

for agent, subtask in zip(agents, subtasks):
    agent.execute_subtask(subtask)
```

Here, tasks are decomposed and distributed among agents, ensuring parallel execution.

4. Efficient Communication Protocols

Designing lightweight communication protocols ensures that agents exchange only necessary information, reducing network congestion.

Example:

Instead of broadcasting updates to all agents, agents can communicate only with their immediate neighbors or use event-driven messages triggered by specific conditions.

Real-World Examples

1. Amazon's Robotic Warehouses

In Amazon's fulfillment centers, thousands of robots operate simultaneously, picking items and delivering them to human workers. To manage scalability, robots communicate locally to avoid collisions, while high-level systems handle global coordination.

2. Smart Grid Energy Distribution

In smart grids, energy producers, consumers, and storage systems act as agents. Localized decision-making allows neighborhoods to balance energy needs efficiently, while high-level agents oversee the grid's stability.

Scalability and complexity are fundamental challenges in multi-agent system design, but they can be managed through hierarchical architectures, decentralized decision-making, task decomposition, and efficient communication. By implementing these strategies, MAS can handle large-scale operations without compromising performance.

6.2 Ethical Considerations in MAS Development

Multi-agent systems (MAS) have the power to transform industries, enhance decision-making, and solve complex problems. However, with this power comes the responsibility to ensure that MAS are developed and deployed ethically. Decisions made by autonomous agents can have far-reaching consequences, and it is essential to address issues like fairness, accountability, transparency, and the societal impact of these systems.

The Importance of Ethics in MAS

When agents operate autonomously, they often interact with humans and influence decisions that can impact lives, finances, and even the environment. Ethical concerns arise because:

MAS decisions may unintentionally reflect biases in the data they are trained on.

Autonomous agents may prioritize efficiency over fairness, causing harm.

Transparency issues can make it hard for humans to understand or trust MAS.

Addressing these challenges is not optional—it is critical to ensuring that MAS benefit society as a whole.

Key Ethical Challenges in MAS

1. Bias in Decision-Making

Bias is one of the most pervasive ethical challenges in MAS. When agents are trained on biased datasets, their decisions can perpetuate or amplify those biases. For example, a hiring MAS trained on historical data may favor certain demographics while discriminating against others.

Example: Bias in Loan Approval

Imagine an agent tasked with approving loans based on applicant data. If the training data contains historical biases (e.g., rejecting loans for applicants from certain regions), the agent may replicate these biases, leading to unfair outcomes.

Code Example: Detecting Bias

```python
class LoanApprovalAgent:
    def __init__(self, training_data):
        self.training_data = training_data

    def detect_bias(self):
        region_counts = {}
        for entry in self.training_data:
            region = entry["region"]
            if region not in region_counts:
                region_counts[region] = 0
            region_counts[region] += 1

        # Check for imbalance in regions
        for region, count in region_counts.items():
            print(f"Region {region}: {count}
applications")

# Example training data
data = [
    {"region": "A", "approved": True},
    {"region": "B", "approved": False},
    {"region": "A", "approved": True},
    {"region": "B", "approved": False},
]

agent = LoanApprovalAgent(data)
agent.detect_bias()
```

In this example:

The agent analyzes its training data to detect regional biases.

Developers can address these biases by ensuring balanced and fair datasets.

2. Transparency and Explainability

MAS decisions can seem like a "black box" to users, especially when agents use complex algorithms like neural networks. Lack of explainability makes it difficult for humans to trust the system, particularly in high-stakes scenarios such as healthcare or legal decisions.

Example: Medical Diagnosis

A medical diagnosis agent might recommend a treatment plan, but if it cannot explain why, doctors and patients may hesitate to follow its advice.

Code Example: Explainable AI

class Diagnosis Agent:

```python
    def __init__(self):
        self.rules = {
            "fever": "Prescribe antipyretic",
            "cough": "Prescribe cough suppressant",
        }

    def diagnose(self, symptoms):
        for symptom in symptoms:
            if symptom in self.rules:
                return self.rules[symptom],
f"Reason: Detected {symptom}."
        return "Perform further tests", "Reason:
Symptoms unclear."

# Simulate diagnosis
agent = DiagnosisAgent()
symptoms = ["fever", "cough"]
recommendation, explanation =
agent.diagnose(symptoms)
print(f"Recommendation: {recommendation}")
print(f"Explanation: {explanation}")
```

This example shows how an agent can provide both a recommendation and an explanation, building user trust.

3. Privacy and Data Security

MAS often handle sensitive data, such as personal health records or financial information. Ensuring that this data remains secure and private is critical to protecting users from harm.

Example: Protecting Healthcare Data

In a hospital, MAS agents might process patient data to optimize schedules or recommend treatments. Without robust encryption, this data could be intercepted or misused.

Code Example: Encrypting Communication

```python
from cryptography.fernet import Fernet

# Generate an encryption key
key = Fernet.generate_key()
cipher = Fernet(key)

class SecureAgent:
    def __init__(self, name):
        self.name = name

    def send_message(self, recipient, message):
        encrypted_message =
cipher.encrypt(message.encode())
        print(f"{self.name} to {recipient.name}:
{encrypted_message}")
        recipient.receive_message(encrypted_message
)

    def receive_message(self, encrypted_message):
        decrypted_message =
cipher.decrypt(encrypted_message).decode()
        print(f"{self.name} received:
{decrypted_message}")

# Simulate secure communication
agent1 = SecureAgent("Agent-1")
agent2 = SecureAgent("Agent-2")

agent1.send_message(agent2, "Patient data processed
successfully.")
```

This example demonstrates how to secure agent communication using encryption, ensuring data privacy.

4. Accountability and Responsibility

When an MAS makes a mistake, determining who is accountable can be challenging. For instance, if an autonomous vehicle causes an accident, is the fault with the developer, the manufacturer, or the vehicle itself?

Mitigating Accountability Issues

Define clear guidelines for agent behavior.

Maintain detailed logs of agent actions to trace decision-making processes.

Real-World Example: Ethical MAS in Autonomous Vehicles

Autonomous vehicles (AVs) must make life-and-death decisions, such as how to respond to an imminent collision. These decisions raise ethical questions:

Should the AV prioritize passenger safety or pedestrian safety?

How can we ensure that AVs do not discriminate based on factors like age or location?

To address these issues:

Developers use diverse datasets to train AVs.

Decision-making algorithms are tested extensively in simulated environments.

Transparency is ensured by logging and reviewing every decision the AV makes.

Best Practices for Ethical MAS Development

Data Audits: Regularly review datasets for biases and imbalances.

Human Oversight: Allow humans to review and override agent decisions when necessary.

Explainable AI: Design agents that can justify their actions clearly.

Privacy by Design: Incorporate security measures into every stage of MAS development.

Ethical considerations are not just an afterthought in MAS development— they are a foundational requirement. By addressing bias, promoting transparency, protecting privacy, and ensuring accountability, developers can create MAS that are not only powerful but also fair and trustworthy. The examples and strategies shared here provide a roadmap for building MAS that align with ethical principles, empowering you to design systems that truly benefit society.

6.3 Ensuring Security and Privacy

In a world increasingly driven by multi-agent systems (MAS), ensuring security and privacy is not just an option—it's a necessity. MAS often operate in environments where sensitive data is processed, decisions are made autonomously, and agents communicate continuously. Without robust security and privacy measures, these systems become vulnerable to attacks, data breaches, and misuse, undermining trust and functionality.

Multi-agent systems face unique security and privacy challenges because of their distributed and autonomous nature. Let's break down some of the key challenges:

1. Vulnerability to Attacks

In MAS, agents communicate over networks, making them susceptible to various types of attacks, such as interception, spoofing, and denial-of-service (DoS). For example, in a smart grid, a malicious actor could intercept communication between energy management agents to disrupt power distribution.

2. Data Privacy Risks

Agents often handle sensitive information, such as personal health data, financial transactions, or location data. Without proper safeguards, unauthorized parties could access or misuse this information.

3. Insider Threats

Not all threats come from external sources. A compromised agent within the system can disrupt operations, leak sensitive data, or act maliciously.

4. Scalability and Security

As the number of agents increases, so does the complexity of securing their interactions. Ensuring that security mechanisms scale effectively without becoming a bottleneck is a significant challenge.

Strategies for Ensuring Security and Privacy

To address these challenges, MAS must incorporate robust security and privacy measures at every level, from communication protocols to data storage and decision-making processes.

1. Secure Communication Between Agents

Agents rely on communication to share information and coordinate tasks. Securing this communication ensures that messages are not intercepted or tampered with.

Encryption

Encryption is a fundamental technique for securing agent communication. Messages are encoded using a key and can only be decoded by the intended recipient.

Code Example: Secure Message Exchange

Here's an example of encrypting communication between agents:

```python
from cryptography.fernet import Fernet

# Generate a key for encryption
key = Fernet.generate_key()
cipher = Fernet(key)

class SecureAgent:
    def __init__(self, name):
        self.name = name

    def send_message(self, recipient, message):
        encrypted_message =
cipher.encrypt(message.encode())
```

```python
            print(f"{self.name} to {recipient.name}:
{encrypted_message}")
            recipient.receive_message(encrypted_message
)

    def receive_message(self, encrypted_message):
            decrypted_message =
cipher.decrypt(encrypted_message).decode()
            print(f"{self.name} received:
{decrypted_message}")

# Simulate secure communication
agent1 = SecureAgent("Agent-1")
agent2 = SecureAgent("Agent-2")

agent1.send_message(agent2, "Secure communication
established.")
```

In this example:

Messages are encrypted before being sent and decrypted upon receipt.

This ensures that even if the message is intercepted, it remains unreadable without the decryption key.

2. Authentication Mechanisms

Authentication ensures that only authorized agents can join the system or access sensitive information. This prevents malicious entities from impersonating legitimate agents.

Example: Agent Authentication

In a networked MAS, agents can use digital certificates or tokens to verify their identity.

3. Privacy-Preserving Computation

In many MAS applications, agents need to process sensitive data without revealing it to other agents. Privacy-preserving techniques like homomorphic encryption allow agents to compute on encrypted data without decrypting it.

4. Monitoring and Anomaly Detection

To address insider threats, MAS can include monitoring agents that detect unusual behaviors. For instance, if an agent starts sending an unusually high volume of messages, it might indicate that the agent has been compromised.

5. Robust Consensus Mechanisms

In decentralized systems, consensus mechanisms ensure that decisions are not controlled by a single agent or a small group of malicious agents.

Example: Blockchain for MAS

Blockchain technology can provide a secure, immutable ledger for MAS. For example, in supply chain MAS, blockchain ensures transparency and trust by recording every transaction between agents.

Real-World Examples of Security and Privacy in MAS

1. Healthcare Applications

In telemedicine systems, MAS agents handle patient data, schedule appointments, and recommend treatments. Ensuring that this data remains secure is critical to maintaining patient trust.

Implementation

Agents encrypt patient data before storing or transmitting it.

Authentication mechanisms verify the identity of healthcare professionals accessing the data.

2. Autonomous Vehicles

Autonomous vehicles act as agents, sharing data like location, speed, and traffic conditions. Securing this communication prevents malicious actors from sending false data that could cause accidents.

Implementation

V2V (vehicle-to-vehicle) communication is encrypted to prevent interception.

Anomaly detection identifies and isolates compromised vehicles.

3. Smart Grids

In smart grids, MAS agents manage energy distribution, monitor usage, and balance supply and demand. A cyberattack on the grid could disrupt power for entire regions.

Implementation

Distributed authentication ensures only authorized agents participate in the grid.

Blockchain records energy transactions, ensuring transparency and preventing tampering.

Exercise: Implementing a Secure MAS

```
Here's an exercise where agents communicate
securely and verify each other's identity before
sharing sensitive information:
from cryptography.fernet import Fernet

# Generate a key for encryption
key = Fernet.generate_key()
cipher = Fernet(key)

class SecureAgent:
    def __init__(self, name, auth_token):
        self.name = name
        self.auth_token = auth_token

    def authenticate(self, token):
        return self.auth_token == token

    def send_message(self, recipient, message,
token):
        if recipient.authenticate(token):
            encrypted_message =
cipher.encrypt(message.encode())
            print(f"{self.name} to
{recipient.name}: {encrypted_message}")
            recipient.receive_message(encrypted_mes
sage)
        else:
            print(f"{self.name}: Authentication
failed for {recipient.name}.")
```

```
def receive_message(self, encrypted_message):
    decrypted_message =
cipher.decrypt(encrypted_message).decode()
    print(f"{self.name} received:
{decrypted_message}")

# Create agents with authentication tokens
agent1 = SecureAgent("Agent-1", "token123")
agent2 = SecureAgent("Agent-2", "token123")

# Secure communication with authentication
agent1.send_message(agent2, "Secure transaction
complete.", "token123")
```

Security and privacy are foundational to the success and trustworthiness of multi-agent systems. By employing techniques like encryption, authentication, and privacy-preserving computation, you can design MAS that protect sensitive data, resist attacks, and maintain integrity. The examples and exercises provided here offer practical guidance for addressing these challenges, ensuring that your MAS is not only powerful but also secure and private.

Chapter 7: Tools and Frameworks for Developing Multi-Agent Systems

Developing a multi-agent system (MAS) requires the right tools and frameworks to streamline design, implementation, and testing. With advancements in software engineering and artificial intelligence, numerous platforms, libraries, and simulation environments have been created to support MAS development. These tools simplify the complex task of building systems where multiple autonomous agents collaborate, learn, and adapt. In this chapter, I will walk you through some of the most widely used platforms, programming languages, libraries, and simulation environments for MAS development.

7.1 Overview of MAS Development Platforms

When you're developing a multi-agent system (MAS), choosing the right platform can make the process significantly smoother. A development platform provides the tools, libraries, and infrastructure you need to build, manage, and deploy agents in a structured and efficient way. These platforms often include built-in support for agent communication, coordination, and execution, saving you the trouble of coding everything from scratch.

MAS development platforms are software environments designed to facilitate the creation of systems where agents interact autonomously. These platforms provide a foundation for:

Communication: Agents need to exchange information seamlessly. Platforms often include protocols and APIs for this.

Coordination: Agents must work together efficiently. Platforms help with task allocation, negotiation, and consensus mechanisms.

Execution: Platforms manage agent lifecycles, from creation to termination.

By handling these foundational aspects, platforms allow you to focus on building the unique logic and behaviors of your agents.

Popular MAS Development Platforms

Let's explore some of the most trusted platforms for MAS development. Each has its own strengths, and I'll guide you on when and why to use them.

1. JADE (Java Agent DEvelopment Framework)

JADE is one of the most established platforms for MAS development. Built in Java, it provides a structured framework for creating agents and managing their interactions. JADE is particularly powerful for large-scale distributed systems, as it simplifies the complexities of communication and coordination.

Key Features

FIPA Compliance: JADE adheres to FIPA (Foundation for Intelligent Physical Agents) standards, ensuring that your agents can communicate with agents from other systems.

Built-in Messaging: It provides an easy-to-use API for sending and receiving messages between agents.

Agent Management: JADE simplifies the creation, registration, and lifecycle management of agents.

Real-World Example: Logistics System

A logistics company uses JADE to coordinate delivery vehicles. Each vehicle is an agent that communicates with others to optimize delivery routes, avoid traffic, and redistribute packages dynamically in case of delays.

Code Example: Creating a JADE Agent

Here's a basic example of creating an agent in JADE:

```
import jade.core.Agent;

public class SimpleAgent extends Agent {
    @Override
    protected void setup() {
        System.out.println("Hello! I am an agent.
My name is " + getLocalName());
    }
}
```

In this example:

The setup method initializes the agent.

The agent prints its name when it starts.

2. NetLogo

NetLogo is widely used in research and education for modeling and simulating MAS. It's ideal for visualizing systems with many simple agents that interact in a shared environment.

Key Features

User-Friendly Interface: NetLogo has a straightforward interface that makes it easy to design and visualize agent behaviors.

Built-In Models: It comes with a library of pre-built models for common MAS scenarios like traffic simulations or ecological systems.

Real-World Example: Disease Spread Simulation

Public health researchers use NetLogo to simulate how a disease spreads through a population. Each individual in the population is an agent, and their interactions determine the spread rate.

Code Example: Agent Movement in NetLogo

In NetLogo, you can simulate agent movement like this:

```
turtles-own [energy]

to setup
  clear-all
  create-turtles 10 [
    setxy random-xcor random-ycor
    set energy random 100
  ]
  reset-ticks
end

to go
  ask turtles [
    move
    check-energy
  ]
```

```
   tick
end

to move
   forward 1
end

to check-energy
   if energy < 10 [
      set color red
   ]
end
```

Here:

Agents (called "turtles") move randomly on a grid.

They change color to red when their energy level drops below a threshold.

3. GAMA Platform

GAMA is a powerful, open-source platform designed for modeling and simulating complex MAS. It's particularly effective for systems where agents operate across multiple scales or interact with geospatial data.

Key Features

Multi-Scale Modeling: GAMA allows you to define agents that operate at different levels (e.g., individuals, groups, environments).

GIS Integration: It supports geospatial data, making it ideal for urban planning or ecological simulations.

Flexible Scripting: Agents can be programmed using a custom scripting language.

Real-World Example: Urban Traffic Simulation

Urban planners use GAMA to simulate how changes in road infrastructure affect traffic flow. Agents representing vehicles and pedestrians interact with each other and the environment.

4. Any Logic

Any Logic is a commercial simulation tool that supports agent-based, discrete-event, and system dynamics modeling. It's widely used in industries like manufacturing, logistics, and healthcare.

Key Features

Drag-and-Drop Interface: You can design agent behaviors visually, reducing the need for complex coding.

Integration with Data: Any Logic allows you to import real-world data to create realistic simulations.

Scalability: It's capable of simulating large-scale systems with thousands of agents.

Real-World Example: Hospital Resource Optimization

A hospital uses Any Logic to simulate patient flow and staff allocation, ensuring that resources are used efficiently during peak hours.

How to Choose the Right Platform

Selecting the right MAS development platform depends on your specific needs:

For Research and Education: Net Logo is a great choice for simple, visual simulations.

For Large-Scale Systems: JADE is ideal for building scalable, distributed MAS.

For Complex Models with Geospatial Data: GAMA provides advanced capabilities for multi-scale simulations.

For Industry Applications: Any Logic offers powerful tools for modeling and optimizing real-world systems.

MAS development platforms are the backbone of modern multi-agent systems. They simplify the process of creating, managing, and simulating agents, allowing you to focus on the unique challenges of your project. From JADE's robust communication tools to NetLogo's user-friendly simulations, these platforms empower you to build systems that are both powerful and efficient.

7.2 Programming Languages and Libraries

When building multi-agent systems (MAS), your choice of programming language and libraries is critical. These tools shape how you design, implement, and test your system. Each language and library has strengths tailored to different types of projects, from large-scale distributed systems to simple simulations.

MAS often involve tasks like communication, decision-making, coordination, and data handling. The programming language you choose needs to support these functionalities effectively. Key factors include:

Ease of use: A language that's easy to learn allows you to focus on the logic of your agents rather than wrestling with syntax.

Performance: For systems requiring real-time interaction, performance is critical.

Library and community support: Libraries save time by providing pre-built tools for common MAS tasks, and a strong community ensures you have resources when you encounter challenges.

Popular Programming Languages for MAS

1. Python

Python is a versatile and beginner-friendly language that has gained immense popularity in MAS development. It's particularly well-suited for prototyping, simulations, and agent-based modeling due to its simplicity and extensive libraries.

Key Libraries for MAS in Python

1. Mesa
 Mesa is a Python library specifically designed for agent-based modeling. It simplifies the creation of agents and their environments while providing tools for visualization.

Practical Example: Building a Simple MAS with Mesa

Let's create a basic simulation where agents move randomly on a grid:

```
from mesa import Agent, Model
```

```python
from mesa.time import RandomActivation
from mesa.space import MultiGrid

class RandomAgent(Agent):
    def __init__(self, unique_id, model):
        super().__init__(unique_id, model)

    def step(self):
        # Move the agent to a random neighboring cell
        possible_steps =
        self.model.grid.get_neighborhood(self.pos,
        moore=True, include_center=False)
        new_position =
        self.random.choice(possible_steps)
        self.model.grid.move_agent(self,
        new_position)

class RandomModel(Model):
    def __init__(self, num_agents, width, height):
        self.num_agents = num_agents
        self.grid = MultiGrid(width, height, True)
        self.schedule = RandomActivation(self)

        for i in range(self.num_agents):
            agent = RandomAgent(i, self)
            self.schedule.add(agent)
            self.grid.place_agent(agent,
        (self.random.randrange(width),
        self.random.randrange(height)))

    def step(self):
        self.schedule.step()

# Create and run the model
model = RandomModel(10, 10, 10)
for i in range(5):   # Simulate 5 steps
    model.step()
```

Here:

Each agent moves randomly within a grid.

Mesa handles agent scheduling, movement, and interaction.

DEAP (Distributed Evolutionary Algorithms in Python)
DEAP is used to implement evolutionary algorithms in MAS, allowing agents to learn and adapt.

2. Java

Java is a powerful choice for large-scale, distributed MAS. Its performance, platform independence, and robust concurrency model make it ideal for complex systems requiring agent communication and coordination.

Key Framework for MAS in Java

JADE (Java Agent DEvelopment Framework)
JADE simplifies the creation of FIPA-compliant agents, enabling them to communicate and coordinate seamlessly.

Practical Example: Basic Agent in JADE

Below is an example of a simple JADE agent:

```
import jade.core.Agent;

public class HelloAgent extends Agent {
    @Override
    protected void setup() {
        System.out.println("Hello! My name is " +
getLocalName());
    }
}
```

When you run this code:

The JADE platform initializes the agent.

The setup method is called, allowing you to define the agent's behavior.

JADE also supports complex tasks like negotiation, task allocation, and distributed execution.

3. C++

C++ is commonly used in MAS where performance is critical, such as robotics or real-time systems. Its ability to manage memory and execute low-level operations efficiently makes it a preferred choice for hardware-focused applications.

Real-World Use Case: Swarm Robotics

In swarm robotics, agents (robots) must coordinate in real time to achieve tasks like search-and-rescue or formation control. C++ enables precise control over hardware interactions and sensor data processing.

4. JavaScript

JavaScript is gaining traction in MAS development for web-based simulations and visualizations. With libraries like **Three.js** or **D3.js**, you can create interactive and visually appealing agent-based models directly in a browser.

Example Use Case

An e-commerce platform uses a JavaScript-based MAS to model customer behavior and optimize recommendation algorithms in real time.

5. R

R is widely used for statistical modeling and data-driven agent simulations. While it's not a general-purpose programming language, R excels in scenarios requiring heavy data analysis.

Example Use Case

Social scientists use R to simulate and analyze social networks, where each individual is an agent.

Choosing the Right Language

Your choice of language depends on the specific needs of your project:

Use **Python** if you prioritize simplicity, visualization, or rapid prototyping.

Opt for **Java** if you need a scalable and robust solution for distributed MAS.

Go with **C++** if performance and hardware integration are critical.

Leverage **JavaScript** for web-based, interactive simulations.

Choose **R** for data-centric agent simulations.

Libraries for MAS-Specific Functions

In addition to general programming languages, several libraries are designed to support MAS development. Here are a few worth exploring:

MASON: A Java-based library for large-scale simulations.

Repast: A flexible, agent-based modeling toolkit.

PySC2: A Python library for MAS in reinforcement learning, especially for StarCraft II environments.

Programming languages and libraries are the backbone of MAS development, shaping how agents are built, interact, and function. Python's simplicity makes it ideal for prototyping and simulations, while Java's robustness is perfect for scalable and distributed systems. For performance-critical applications, C++ excels, and JavaScript opens up opportunities for interactive, browser-based models. With the right language and tools, you can build MAS tailored to your project's needs, whether you're simulating social behavior or coordinating robotic swarms.

7.3 Simulation Environments for MAS

Simulation is a critical step in the development and evaluation of multi-agent systems (MAS). It allows developers to test agent behaviors, interactions, and overall system performance in a controlled environment before deployment. A robust simulation environment can help you visualize how agents interact, understand emergent behaviors, and identify potential bottlenecks or conflicts.

Why Simulate MAS?

Before deploying an MAS in the real world, you need to ensure that it operates as expected. Simulation environments allow you to:

Test agent behaviors: Ensure that agents follow their programmed logic and achieve their goals.

Observe interactions: Identify how agents cooperate, compete, or conflict with each other.

Evaluate performance: Measure the system's efficiency, scalability, and adaptability under different conditions.

Mitigate risks: Avoid costly mistakes by identifying and addressing issues early.

Simulation environments provide the tools to achieve all this, often including visualization, performance metrics, and debugging features.

Popular Simulation Environments for MAS

1. NetLogo

NetLogo is one of the most user-friendly simulation environments for MAS. It is ideal for modeling systems where many simple agents interact, making it perfect for social simulations, ecological studies, and educational projects.

Key Features

Agent-based modeling: Every agent (called a "turtle") can independently follow its own logic.

Built-in visualization: NetLogo provides a graphical interface to observe agent interactions in real time.

Ease of use: Its programming language is straightforward, even for beginners.

Real-World Example

Researchers use NetLogo to study the spread of diseases in a population. Each person is represented as an agent with properties like immunity and social behavior, allowing researchers to test different intervention strategies.

Code Example: Basic Movement Simulation

Here's how you can create a simple simulation in NetLogo where agents move randomly:

```
turtles-own [energy]

to setup
  clear-all
  create-turtles 100 [
    setxy random-xcor random-ycor
```

```
      set energy random 100
  ]
  reset-ticks
end

to go
  ask turtles [
    move
    check-energy
  ]
  tick
end

to move
  forward 1
end

to check-energy
  if energy < 10 [
    set color red
  ]
end
```

In this simulation:

100 agents are created and move randomly across the grid.

Agents with low energy turn red, helping you visualize their state.

2. Mesa (Python)

Mesa is a Python-based framework for agent-based modeling. It combines Python's simplicity with powerful tools for modeling and visualization, making it a favorite among developers and researchers.

Key Features

Scalability: Mesa handles simulations with hundreds or thousands of agents.

Interactive visualization: It provides tools to observe agent behaviors in real time.

Customizable: Python's flexibility allows you to integrate Mesa with other libraries like NumPy or Pandas.

Real-World Example

Urban planners use Mesa to simulate traffic flow in a city. Vehicles and pedestrians are represented as agents that interact with each other and their environment, enabling planners to test new road layouts or traffic light timings.

Code Example: Grid-Based Movement with Mesa

```python
from mesa import Agent, Model

from mesa.time import RandomActivation

from mesa.space import MultiGrid


class MovingAgent(Agent):
    def __init__(self, unique_id, model):
        super().__init__(unique_id, model)


    def step(self):
        possible_steps      =      self.model.grid.get_neighborhood(self.pos, moore=True, include_center=False)
        new_position = self.random.choice(possible_steps)
        self.model.grid.move_agent(self, new_position)


class MovementModel(Model):
    def __init__(self, num_agents, width, height):
        self.num_agents = num_agents
        self.grid = MultiGrid(width, height, True)
```

```python
        self.schedule = RandomActivation(self)

        for i in range(self.num_agents):
            agent = MovingAgent(i, self)
            self.schedule.add(agent)
            self.grid.place_agent(agent,        (self.random.randrange(width),
self.random.randrange(height)))

    def step(self):
        self.schedule.step()


# Run the simulation
model = MovementModel(10, 10, 10)
for i in range(10):
    model.step()
```

This Python script creates agents that move randomly within a grid, similar to the NetLogo example but with Python's versatility.

3. GAMA Platform

GAMA is an advanced simulation platform for complex systems. It excels in multi-scale modeling, allowing you to simulate systems where agents operate at different levels (e.g., individual, group, and environment).

Key Features

GIS Integration: GAMA supports geospatial data, making it ideal for simulations involving real-world locations.

Scalable visualization: Simulations can be viewed in both 2D and 3D.

Custom scripting: GAML (GAMA Modeling Language) provides flexibility for defining agent behaviors.

Real-World Example

Disaster response teams use GAMA to simulate evacuation scenarios in urban areas. Agents represent individuals, vehicles, and emergency services, allowing teams to optimize evacuation plans.

4. AnyLogic

AnyLogic is a commercial simulation platform that supports agent-based, discrete-event, and system dynamics modeling. It is widely used in industries like logistics, healthcare, and manufacturing.

Key Features

Drag-and-drop modeling: You can design agent behaviors visually, making it accessible even to non-programmers.

Data integration: AnyLogic allows you to incorporate real-world data into your simulations.

High-performance simulations: It can handle large-scale systems with thousands of agents.

Real-World Example

A supply chain company uses AnyLogic to model warehouse operations, testing different strategies for inventory management and order fulfillment.

5. Unity3D

Unity3D is a game development engine that has found a place in MAS simulation due to its powerful 3D capabilities. It's especially useful for robotics, gaming, and virtual reality applications.

Key Features

3D environments: Create realistic simulations with detailed visuals.

Real-time interaction: Simulate agent behaviors and observe outcomes dynamically.

Extensibility: Unity3D supports plugins and custom scripts for added functionality.

Real-World Example

A robotics lab uses Unity3D to simulate swarm robotics, testing algorithms for coordination and collision avoidance in a virtual environment before deploying them in real-world robots.

How to Choose the Right Simulation Environment

Choosing the right simulation environment depends on your project's requirements:

Use **NetLogo** if you need a simple, visual tool for education or research.

Choose **Mesa** if you prefer Python and need flexibility or scalability.

Opt for **GAMA** if your project involves geospatial data or multi-scale modeling.

Consider **AnyLogic** for industrial applications like logistics or healthcare.

Leverage **Unity3D** for visually rich simulations, especially in robotics or virtual environments.

Simulation environments are indispensable for testing and refining MAS. They provide a safe space to observe agent interactions, test strategies, and identify potential issues. Platforms like NetLogo, Mesa, GAMA, AnyLogic, and Unity3D cater to a wide range of use cases, from academic research to industrial applications. The practical examples shared here give you a starting point for exploring these tools and choosing the one that best fits your needs. With the right simulation environment, you can bring your MAS ideas to life and ensure they're ready for real-world deployment.

Chapter 8: Emerging Trends and Future Directions in MAS

The field of multi-agent systems (MAS) continues to evolve, influenced by advancements in artificial intelligence, blockchain, quantum computing, and other cutting-edge technologies. These emerging trends are shaping the future of MAS, expanding their capabilities, and unlocking new possibilities across industries.

8.1 Integrating MAS with Artificial Intelligence

The integration of artificial intelligence (AI) with multi-agent systems (MAS) is a transformative development that takes MAS to the next level. By combining the decentralized coordination of MAS with the cognitive capabilities of AI, we create systems that are not only autonomous but also intelligent, adaptive, and capable of solving complex problems in dynamic environments.

Why Integrate AI with MAS?

MAS are inherently distributed, with agents operating autonomously while coordinating with one another to achieve shared goals. However, traditional MAS rely on predefined rules and decision-making frameworks. Integrating AI into MAS enables agents to:

Learn from data: Instead of being constrained by static rules, agents can adapt based on patterns in the data they encounter.

Make better decisions: AI allows agents to predict outcomes and optimize their strategies.

Handle uncertainty: AI techniques like probabilistic reasoning enable agents to make informed decisions even with incomplete information.

Collaborate effectively: AI-powered agents can negotiate, plan, and cooperate in more sophisticated ways.

AI Techniques That Enhance MAS

Let's break down some of the AI techniques commonly used in MAS and how they enhance agent capabilities.

1. Machine Learning for Adaptive Agents

Machine learning enables agents to learn from data and improve their performance over time. This is particularly useful in environments where conditions change dynamically, such as stock markets or supply chains.

Example: Predicting Demand in a Supply Chain

Imagine a supply chain MAS where each warehouse is an agent responsible for managing its inventory. Using machine learning, the agents can predict demand based on historical sales data, seasonal trends, and external factors.

Code Example: A Simple Prediction Model

```python
from sklearn.linear_model import LinearRegression
import numpy as np

# Historical demand data (input features) and sales
(labels)
data = np.array([[1], [2], [3], [4], [5]])   # Weeks
sales = np.array([100, 150, 200, 250, 300])   #
Units sold

# Train a simple linear regression model
model = LinearRegression().fit(data, sales)

class WarehouseAgent:
    def __init__(self, model):
        self.model = model

    def predict_demand(self, week):
        prediction = self.model.predict([[week]])
        return prediction[0]

# Create an AI-powered agent
warehouse = WarehouseAgent(model)
week = 6
predicted_sales = warehouse.predict_demand(week)
print(f"Predicted sales for week {week}:
{predicted_sales:.2f} units")
```

In this example:

The agent predicts sales for the upcoming week using a machine learning model.

This allows the warehouse to plan inventory and avoid overstocking or shortages.

2. Reinforcement Learning for Decision-Making

Reinforcement learning (RL) is a type of machine learning where agents learn by interacting with their environment and receiving feedback in the form of rewards or penalties. This is ideal for MAS where agents need to optimize their strategies through trial and error.

Example: Traffic Light Optimization

In a smart traffic system, each traffic light is an agent. Using RL, the lights learn to optimize their timings based on traffic flow, reducing congestion and travel times.

Code Example: Reinforcement Learning with Q-Learning

```python
import numpy as np

class TrafficLightAgent:
    def __init__(self, actions):
        self.q_table = {}
        self.actions = actions

    def choose_action(self, state):
        if state not in self.q_table:
            self.q_table[state] =
np.zeros(len(self.actions))
        return np.argmax(self.q_table[state])

    def update_q_value(self, state, action, reward,
next_state, alpha, gamma):
        if next_state not in self.q_table:
            self.q_table[next_state] =
np.zeros(len(self.actions))
        best_next_action =
np.argmax(self.q_table[next_state])
        self.q_table[state][action] += alpha * (
```

```
                reward + gamma *
self.q_table[next_state][best_next_action] -
self.q_table[state][action]
        )

# Simulating a traffic light agent
actions = ["extend green", "shorten green"]
agent = TrafficLightAgent(actions)
state = "low traffic"
action = agent.choose_action(state)
print(f"Action taken: {actions[action]}")
```

In this example:

The agent learns optimal actions based on rewards (e.g., reduced congestion).

Q-learning updates the agent's knowledge over time.

3. Natural Language Processing (NLP) for Communication

NLP enables agents to understand and generate human language, facilitating interaction with humans and other agents.

Example: Customer Service Chatbot

In an MAS for customer service, chatbots act as agents that answer common questions while escalating complex queries to human agents. NLP techniques allow the chatbots to understand user queries and provide relevant responses.

Code Example: Simple Chatbot

```
from transformers import pipeline

# Load a pre-trained question-answering model
qa_pipeline = pipeline("question-answering")

class ChatbotAgent:
    def __init__(self, qa_pipeline):
        self.qa_pipeline = qa_pipeline

    def respond(self, question, context):
```

```
        answer =
self.qa_pipeline(question=question,
context=context)
        return answer["answer"]

# Example usage
chatbot = ChatbotAgent(qa_pipeline)
context = "Our office is open from 9 AM to 5 PM,
Monday to Friday."
question = "What are your office hours?"
response = chatbot.respond(question, context)
print(f"Chatbot Response: {response}")
```

This example shows how an agent uses an NLP model to answer questions based on context.

4. Computer Vision for Perception

Computer vision enables agents to interpret visual data from cameras or sensors. This is essential for applications like autonomous vehicles, drones, or robotic systems.

Example: Drones in Disaster Response

In a disaster-response MAS, drones equipped with computer vision can detect survivors, assess damage, and coordinate rescue efforts.

Real-World Applications

1. Smart Cities

MAS powered by AI are revolutionizing urban systems. For example:

Traffic agents optimize flow based on real-time data.

Energy agents in smart grids balance supply and demand efficiently.

2. Healthcare

In healthcare, MAS with AI support personalized treatment plans, automate scheduling, and monitor patients using wearable devices.

3. Financial Markets

AI-powered agents in financial MAS analyze market data, predict trends, and execute trades autonomously.

Integrating artificial intelligence with multi-agent systems unlocks new levels of autonomy, adaptability, and intelligence. From machine learning and reinforcement learning to natural language processing and computer vision, AI empowers agents to learn, adapt, and make smarter decisions. The examples provided here illustrate the practical benefits and applications of this integration, helping you envision how to design MAS that leverage AI to solve complex, real-world problems effectively.

8.2 Blockchain and MAS for Trust and Security

When multiple autonomous agents interact in a distributed system, trust and security become fundamental concerns. How can agents verify the authenticity of their counterparts? How do we ensure that interactions between agents are secure and tamper-proof? Blockchain technology addresses these challenges by providing a decentralized, transparent, and immutable ledger that ensures secure and trusted interactions.

Why Blockchain is a Game-Changer for MAS

MAS inherently involve multiple agents working autonomously, often without a central authority. However, this autonomy introduces challenges:

Trust: Agents may interact with unknown or unverified entities.

Security: Communication and transactions can be intercepted or manipulated.

Transparency: Verifying actions and transactions becomes difficult without a central audit mechanism.

Blockchain solves these issues by:

Providing a Shared Ledger: All transactions are recorded in an immutable ledger accessible to all agents.

Ensuring Trustless Verification: Agents can verify the integrity of data and transactions without relying on intermediaries.

Facilitating Smart Contracts: Agreements between agents can be automated, reducing human intervention.

How Blockchain Enhances MAS

Let's break down how blockchain integrates with MAS to enhance their functionality:

1. Decentralized Trust

In traditional systems, a central authority validates transactions. Blockchain eliminates this dependency by enabling agents to validate transactions themselves using consensus mechanisms like Proof of Work (PoW) or Proof of Stake (PoS).

Real-World Example: Decentralized Energy Grids

In a smart energy grid MAS, households equipped with solar panels act as agents that sell surplus energy to others. Blockchain ensures that transactions between agents (households) are secure, verified, and tamper-proof, without relying on a central utility company.

2. Immutable Records

Blockchain creates a permanent record of all interactions between agents. Once a transaction is added to the blockchain, it cannot be altered, ensuring transparency and accountability.

Code Example: Recording Transactions

Here's a Python example that simulates agents recording transactions on a blockchain:

```python
import hashlib
import time

class Blockchain:
    def __init__(self):
        self.chain = []
        self.create_block(previous_hash="0",
data="Genesis Block")

    def create_block(self, previous_hash, data):
```

```python
        block = {
            "index": len(self.chain) + 1,
            "timestamp": time.time(),
            "data": data,
            "previous_hash": previous_hash,
            "hash": self.hash_block(previous_hash,
data),
        }
        self.chain.append(block)
        return block

    def hash_block(self, previous_hash, data):
        block_string =
f"{previous_hash}{data}{time.time()}".encode()
        return
hashlib.sha256(block_string).hexdigest()

# Create a blockchain
blockchain = Blockchain()

# Agent transactions
agent1_data = "Agent-1 sends 10 energy units to
Agent-2"
blockchain.create_block(blockchain.chain[-
1]["hash"], agent1_data)

agent2_data = "Agent-2 sends 5 energy units to
Agent-3"
blockchain.create_block(blockchain.chain[-
1]["hash"], agent2_data)

# Print blockchain
for block in blockchain.chain:
    print(block)
```

This code:

Creates a simple blockchain where agents record their transactions.

Ensures that each transaction is linked to the previous one via hashes, making the ledger immutable.

3. Smart Contracts for Automation

Smart contracts are self-executing agreements stored on the blockchain. They automatically enforce terms when predefined conditions are met, making them ideal for automating agent interactions.

Real-World Example: Supply Chain MAS

In a supply chain MAS, smart contracts could automate payments. For instance, when a shipment arrives at its destination, a smart contract triggers payment to the supplier.

Code Example: Conceptual Smart Contract

Below is a simplified Python simulation of how a smart contract might work:

```python
class SmartContract:
    def __init__(self, condition, action):
        self.condition = condition
        self.action = action

    def execute(self, data):
        if self.condition(data):
            return self.action(data)
        return "Conditions not met"

# Define a smart contract
def condition(data):
    return data["status"] == "delivered"

def action(data):
    return f"Payment of ${data['amount']} sent to {data['supplier']}."

contract = SmartContract(condition, action)

# Simulate an agent triggering the contract
shipment = {"status": "delivered", "amount": 1000, "supplier": "Supplier-1"}
print(contract.execute(shipment))
```

This example demonstrates:

How agents can use smart contracts to automate transactions.

The simplicity of defining conditions and actions.

Applications of Blockchain-Enabled MAS

1. Autonomous Vehicles

In MAS for autonomous vehicles, blockchain ensures that vehicle-to-vehicle (V2V) communication is secure. For example:

Vehicles record data like speed, location, and route on the blockchain.

Smart contracts enforce rules, such as toll payments, based on vehicle movement.

2. Healthcare

In healthcare MAS, blockchain secures patient data while allowing authorized agents (doctors, hospitals) to access it. Each interaction with the data is recorded on the blockchain, ensuring transparency.

3. Decentralized Marketplaces

In decentralized marketplaces, blockchain verifies transactions between buyers and sellers, eliminating fraud and ensuring fair exchanges.

Benefits of Blockchain in MAS

Enhanced Security: Data on the blockchain is encrypted and tamper-proof, protecting agents from malicious attacks.

Transparency: Every transaction is visible and verifiable, fostering trust among agents.

Reduced Costs: Blockchain eliminates intermediaries, reducing overhead costs in MAS.

Interoperability: Blockchain allows agents from different MAS to interact securely.

Challenges and Limitations

While blockchain offers immense benefits, it also comes with challenges:

Scalability: Current blockchain systems struggle to handle high transaction volumes.

Energy Consumption: Some consensus mechanisms, like PoW, are energy-intensive.

Complexity: Integrating blockchain into MAS requires technical expertise.

Blockchain technology is revolutionizing MAS by addressing critical challenges like trust, security, and transparency. Whether it's securing transactions in a decentralized energy grid or enabling smart contracts in a supply chain, blockchain empowers agents to interact autonomously and securely.

8.3 The Role of Quantum Computing in MAS

Quantum computing is one of the most exciting and transformative technologies of our time. It introduces a new computational paradigm that leverages the principles of quantum mechanics to solve problems far beyond the reach of classical computers. When applied to multi-agent systems (MAS), quantum computing has the potential to revolutionize how agents interact, solve problems, and make decisions.

Why Quantum Computing Matters in MAS

Traditional computing methods often struggle with the complex, distributed, and dynamic nature of MAS. Quantum computing addresses these challenges by:

Handling complexity: Quantum computers can process vast amounts of data simultaneously, making them ideal for optimizing large-scale MAS.

Improving decision-making: Quantum algorithms can analyze complex scenarios faster and more efficiently than classical algorithms.

Enhancing security: Quantum cryptography provides unbreakable security for agent communication, ensuring data integrity and privacy.

These capabilities open up possibilities for MAS in domains like logistics, healthcare, autonomous systems, and beyond.

How Quantum Computing Enhances MAS

1. Solving Optimization Problems

Optimization is at the core of many MAS applications. Agents often need to find the best solution from a massive set of possibilities, such as route planning for delivery drones or resource allocation in a smart grid. Classical algorithms may require hours or days to compute optimal solutions, but quantum computing can significantly reduce this time.

Example: Route Optimization

Imagine an MAS for delivery drones where each drone needs to determine the shortest route to deliver packages. As the number of drones and delivery points increases, the problem becomes exponentially harder to solve. Quantum computing, through algorithms like the Quantum Approximate Optimization Algorithm (QAOA), can find near-optimal solutions quickly.

2. Enhancing Agent Collaboration

In MAS, agents collaborate to solve distributed problems. Quantum entanglement—a phenomenon where particles are interconnected regardless of distance—enables faster and more synchronized communication between agents. This can improve coordination in real-time applications, such as autonomous vehicle fleets.

Real-World Example: Traffic Management

In a quantum-enabled MAS for traffic management, each traffic signal acts as an agent. Using quantum computing, the agents collectively calculate optimal timings to minimize congestion, considering real-time data like vehicle density and flow rates.

3. Quantum Machine Learning for Intelligent Agents

Quantum machine learning combines the power of quantum computing with AI to enhance agent intelligence. Agents can use quantum algorithms to process data, identify patterns, and make decisions faster than with classical methods.

Code Example: Quantum Optimization with Qiskit

Let's simulate a simple quantum optimization task using IBM's Qiskit library:

```
from qiskit import Aer, QuantumCircuit, execute
```

```
# Create a quantum circuit for a simple
optimization task
qc = QuantumCircuit(2)
qc.h(0)   # Apply Hadamard gate to create
superposition
qc.cx(0, 1)   # Apply CNOT gate for entanglement
qc.measure_all()

# Simulate the circuit
simulator = Aer.get_backend('qasm_simulator')
job = execute(qc, simulator, shots=1024)
result = job.result()
counts = result.get_counts()

print("Optimization result:", counts)
```

In this example:

The quantum circuit explores multiple states simultaneously.

The results represent the probabilities of different outcomes, which can be used for decision-making.

4. Quantum Cryptography for Agent Communication

Security is a critical concern in MAS, especially when agents exchange sensitive information. Quantum cryptography, based on principles like quantum key distribution (QKD), ensures that communication is secure and tamper-proof. Any attempt to intercept messages would be immediately detectable.

Real-World Example: Securing Healthcare MAS

In a healthcare MAS, agents managing patient data (e.g., wearable devices, doctors, hospitals) can use quantum cryptography to ensure that patient information is transmitted securely.

Applications of Quantum Computing in MAS

1. Supply Chain Optimization

In a supply chain MAS, quantum computing can optimize inventory management, logistics, and production schedules by considering millions of variables simultaneously. For example, agents representing warehouses and factories can coordinate using quantum algorithms to minimize costs and delays.

2. Autonomous Vehicles

Quantum-enabled MAS can improve route planning, collision avoidance, and fleet coordination for autonomous vehicles. By processing data from sensors, traffic signals, and other vehicles, agents can make split-second decisions.

3. Energy Management in Smart Grids

In smart grids, agents representing households, energy producers, and storage systems coordinate to balance supply and demand. Quantum computing allows these agents to optimize energy distribution in real time, even during peak demand.

Challenges and Limitations

While quantum computing offers immense potential, it also faces challenges:

Hardware limitations: Quantum computers are still in their infancy, with limited qubits and stability.

Complexity: Developing quantum algorithms requires specialized expertise.

Integration: Incorporating quantum computing into existing MAS frameworks is not straightforward.

Despite these challenges, the field is rapidly advancing, and practical applications are becoming increasingly feasible.

Future Directions

The integration of quantum computing and MAS is still in its early stages, but several developments are shaping the future:

Hybrid Systems: Combining classical and quantum computing to leverage the strengths of both.

Quantum Internet: A network of quantum computers enabling MAS to perform distributed quantum computations.

Quantum AI Agents: Fully quantum-powered agents capable of solving problems that classical AI cannot.

Quantum computing is poised to revolutionize multi-agent systems by addressing their most challenging problems—optimization, collaboration, and security. From enhancing agent intelligence with quantum machine learning to ensuring secure communication with quantum cryptography, the possibilities are endless. While the technology is still evolving, its potential to transform MAS is undeniable.

Chapter 9: Designing for Revolution

Revolutionizing systems with multi-agent systems (MAS) requires more than just deploying intelligent agents—it demands thoughtful design, strategic implementation, robust evaluation metrics, and a commitment to continuous improvement. This chapter focuses on how to implement MAS effectively, measure their impact, and iteratively enhance them to ensure they remain relevant and impactful in dynamic environments.

9.1 Strategic Implementation of MAS

Implementing a multi-agent system (MAS) is not just about developing agents and deploying them into an environment. It's a strategic process that requires careful planning, alignment with organizational goals, and a deep understanding of both the technical and operational aspects of the system. When done correctly, an MAS can transform the way complex problems are solved, but achieving this requires a structured approach.

Strategic implementation is about creating a system that doesn't just work—it creates measurable value. This involves defining clear goals, understanding the environment, designing the system architecture, and ensuring that the implementation aligns with the needs of stakeholders.

To break it down:

You need to **understand the problem** you're solving.

You must **analyze the environment** where the MAS will operate.

You'll design the **architecture and agent behaviors** to meet specific goals.

Finally, you'll **test, deploy, and monitor** the system to ensure continuous value.

Step-by-Step Guide to Strategic Implementation

1. Define Clear Objectives

Every successful MAS starts with a clear understanding of what it's supposed to achieve. Ask yourself:

What problem are you solving?

Who are the stakeholders?

What outcomes define success?

Example: Optimizing Delivery Routes

In logistics, the objective might be to optimize delivery routes for a fleet of vehicles, reducing fuel costs and delivery times while maintaining customer satisfaction.

2. Analyze the Environment

The environment is the context in which agents operate. Understanding it is crucial because the environment's complexity, constraints, and dynamics shape your MAS design.

Key Questions to Explore:

Is the environment **static** (unchanging) or **dynamic** (changing frequently)?

Do agents operate in a **physical space** (e.g., drones delivering packages) or a **digital space** (e.g., chatbots handling customer queries)?

Are resources limited, and how do agents compete for them?

Example: Disaster Response

In a disaster response MAS, the environment includes factors like the terrain, weather, and available resources like medical supplies or vehicles.

3. Design the MAS Architecture

The architecture determines how agents interact with each other and the environment. There are three common approaches:

Centralized: A central controller coordinates all agents. This is effective for small systems with straightforward tasks.

Decentralized: Agents operate autonomously, coordinating directly with each other. This is ideal for large-scale systems with many agents.

Hybrid: Combines elements of both centralized and decentralized architectures.

Code Example: Hybrid Architecture

Here's a Python example simulating a hybrid MAS for task allocation:

```python
class CentralController:
    def __init__(self):
        self.tasks = []

    def assign_task(self, agents):
        for task in self.tasks:
            for agent in agents:
                if agent.is_available():
                    agent.assign_task(task)
                    break

class Agent:
    def __init__(self, name):
        self.name = name
        self.current_task = None

    def is_available(self):
        return self.current_task is None

    def assign_task(self, task):
        self.current_task = task
        print(f"{self.name} assigned to task: {task}")

# Create a controller and agents
controller = CentralController()
controller.tasks = ["Deliver Package A", "Inspect Site B", "Rescue Victim C"]
agents = [Agent(f"Agent-{i}") for i in range(3)]

# Assign tasks
controller.assign_task(agents)
```

This example shows how a central controller assigns tasks to autonomous agents based on their availability.

4. Develop Agent Behaviors

Agents must have well-defined behaviors that align with the system's goals. This involves specifying:

How agents perceive the environment.

How they make decisions.

How they interact with other agents.

Example: Delivery Drone Behavior

A delivery drone might:

Sense its location and remaining battery.

Communicate with other drones to avoid collisions.

Decide the most efficient route based on traffic data.

Code Exercise: Simple Agent Decision-Making

class Delivery Drone:

```
    def __init__(self, name, battery_level):
        self.name = name
        self.battery_level = battery_level

    def decide_action(self,
distance_to_destination):
        if self.battery_level < 20:
            return "Return to base for recharging"
        elif distance_to_destination > 50:
            return "Request assistance from another
drone"
        else:
            return "Proceed to destination"

# Create a drone and simulate decision-making
drone = DeliveryDrone("Drone-1", 30)
action = drone.decide_action(60)
print(f"{drone.name} action: {action}")
```

This demonstrates how an agent makes decisions based on its internal state (battery level) and external factors (distance to destination).

5. Test in Simulated Environments

Before deploying your MAS in the real world, test it in a simulated environment. Simulations help you:

Validate agent behaviors.

Identify potential bottlenecks.

Optimize system performance.

Example: Traffic Simulation

Use platforms like Mesa or NetLogo to simulate agents interacting in a traffic system, observing how different strategies affect congestion.

6. Deploy and Monitor

Deploying the MAS involves integrating it into its target environment and ensuring that it operates smoothly. Monitoring tools are essential for tracking agent performance, system efficiency, and unexpected behaviors.

Challenges to Strategic Implementation

Strategic implementation is not without challenges. Common obstacles include:

Scalability issues: As the number of agents grows, communication and coordination can become bottlenecks.

Uncertainty: Dynamic environments can introduce unpredictability, requiring agents to adapt continuously.

Stakeholder alignment: Balancing the needs of all stakeholders can be complex, especially in large organizations.

Example: Real-World Failure

In a ride-sharing MAS, agents assigned passengers to drivers without considering traffic patterns. This led to delays and inefficiencies, highlighting the need for comprehensive environmental analysis.

Strategic implementation of an MAS requires more than technical expertise— it demands a thorough understanding of the problem, environment, and stakeholders. By following the steps outlined here, from defining objectives to deploying and monitoring the system, you can design MAS that deliver measurable value.

9.2 Metrics for Measuring Success

Measuring the success of a multi-agent system (MAS) is a critical step in its lifecycle. Without clear metrics, it's impossible to know if the system is meeting its objectives, performing efficiently, or delivering value to stakeholders. Metrics not only validate the effectiveness of the MAS but also provide insights for optimization and improvement.

Why Metrics Are Essential

Metrics provide measurable, quantifiable data to assess how well an MAS is performing. They help answer questions like:

Is the MAS achieving its intended goals?

Are agents functioning as expected?

How efficiently is the system operating under different conditions?

By defining and monitoring these metrics, you ensure that the MAS remains aligned with its objectives and adapts to changes in the environment.

Key Metrics for MAS Success

1. Performance Metrics

Performance metrics assess how effectively the MAS achieves its objectives. These include task completion rates, response times, and throughput.

Task Completion Rate

Task completion rate measures the percentage of tasks successfully completed by agents. It's a direct indicator of how well the MAS is functioning.

Code Example: Calculating Task Completion Rate

class MAS:

```
def __init__(self, agents):
    self.agents = agents
```

```
    def calculate_completion_rate(self):
        completed_tasks = sum(agent.completed_tasks
for agent in self.agents)
        total_tasks = sum(agent.total_tasks for
agent in self.agents)
        return (completed_tasks / total_tasks) *
100 if total_tasks > 0 else 0

class Agent:
    def __init__(self, name, completed_tasks,
total_tasks):
        self.name = name
        self.completed_tasks = completed_tasks
        self.total_tasks = total_tasks

# Simulate agents in an MAS
agents = [
    Agent("Agent-1", 8, 10),
    Agent("Agent-2", 9, 10),
    Agent("Agent-3", 7, 10),
]
mas = MAS(agents)
completion_rate = mas.calculate_completion_rate()
print(f"Task Completion Rate:
{completion_rate:.2f}%")
```

In this example:

Each agent tracks its completed and total tasks.

The system calculates the overall task completion rate, a key metric for evaluating performance.

Response Time

Response time measures how quickly agents react to changes in the environment or requests. Lower response times indicate a more efficient system.

Throughput

Throughput measures how many tasks or interactions the system handles within a given time frame. It's particularly useful for assessing scalability and efficiency.

2. Scalability Metrics

Scalability metrics evaluate how well the MAS performs as the number of agents or tasks increases. These metrics ensure that the system can grow without significant degradation in performance.

Example: Measuring Agent Scalability

Agent scalability can be tested by gradually increasing the number of agents in the system and monitoring performance metrics like response time or task completion rate.

Code Example: Testing Scalability

```python
import time

class ScalableMAS:
    def __init__(self, num_agents):
        self.agents = [f"Agent-{i}" for i in range(num_agents)]

    def simulate(self):
        start_time = time.time()
        for agent in self.agents:
            # Simulate each agent processing a task
            time.sleep(0.01)   # Simulate task duration
        end_time = time.time()
        return len(self.agents) / (end_time - start_time)

# Test scalability with varying agent counts
for num_agents in [10, 50, 100]:
    system = ScalableMAS(num_agents)
    throughput = system.simulate()
    print(f"Throughput with {num_agents} agents: {throughput:.2f} tasks/sec")
```

This script:

Simulates an MAS with a varying number of agents.

Measures how throughput changes as the system scales, revealing potential bottlenecks.

3. Robustness Metrics

Robustness metrics evaluate how well the MAS handles failures or unexpected events. A robust system can recover quickly and maintain functionality even when some agents fail.

Error Recovery Rate

The error recovery rate measures how effectively the system resolves errors and resumes normal operations. For example, in a delivery MAS, how quickly can other agents take over when one drone fails?

Fault Tolerance

Fault tolerance assesses the system's ability to continue functioning when agents or components fail. It's a key metric for critical systems like healthcare or disaster response MAS.

4. Cost Metrics

Cost metrics evaluate the system's resource efficiency and financial impact. These include resource utilization and cost savings.

Resource Utilization

Resource utilization measures how effectively agents use resources like bandwidth, energy, or computational power. High utilization rates indicate efficiency, but excessive usage may signal potential overloads.

Cost Savings

Cost savings quantify the financial benefits of implementing the MAS compared to traditional methods. For example, a warehouse MAS might reduce labor costs by automating inventory management.

5. User Experience Metrics

If the MAS interacts with humans, user satisfaction becomes a critical metric. Surveys, feedback, and usability tests can help measure how well the system meets user needs.

Real-World Application: Traffic Management MAS

Let's consider a traffic management MAS where each traffic signal is an agent. Key metrics for this system could include:

Average Wait Time: Measures the time vehicles spend waiting at intersections.

Traffic Flow Efficiency: Evaluates how well the system minimizes congestion.

Energy Savings: Quantifies the reduction in fuel consumption due to optimized traffic flow.

By monitoring these metrics, city planners can assess the MAS's impact and identify areas for improvement.

Using Metrics for Continuous Improvement

Metrics aren't just for evaluation—they're also tools for refinement. By regularly monitoring metrics, you can:

Identify Bottlenecks: Detect where the system is underperforming.

Prioritize Improvements: Focus on areas with the greatest potential for impact.

Validate Changes: Ensure that updates to the MAS lead to measurable improvements.

Metrics are the backbone of evaluating and improving multi-agent systems. From performance and scalability to robustness and cost-efficiency, these measurable indicators provide a clear picture of how well the system is achieving its goals. By defining and tracking these metrics, you can ensure that your MAS delivers value, adapts to changing conditions, and evolves over time.

9.3 Continuous Improvement of MAS

Designing and deploying a multi-agent system (MAS) is not the end of the journey. Continuous improvement is essential to ensure the system evolves to meet changing requirements, adapts to dynamic environments, and leverages advancements in technology. Whether it's optimizing agent behaviors, enhancing system efficiency, or incorporating new data sources, continuous improvement ensures that your MAS remains effective and relevant.

The Need for Continuous Improvement

MAS operate in environments that are often dynamic and unpredictable. For example:

In a **smart city MAS**, traffic patterns change over time due to new infrastructure or population growth.

In a **logistics MAS**, customer demands and supply chain disruptions can introduce new challenges.

Continuous improvement ensures that your MAS can:

Adapt to environmental changes.

Optimize performance over time.

Incorporate feedback from users and stakeholders.

Leverage technological advancements.

Principles of Continuous Improvement

Continuous improvement in MAS is guided by several core principles:

1. Monitor and Measure

Effective improvement starts with a clear understanding of how the system is performing. Monitoring tools and metrics (as discussed in the previous section) provide the data needed to identify strengths and weaknesses.

Example: Monitoring Agent Performance

In a fleet of autonomous delivery drones, monitoring might track metrics like:

Successful deliveries.

Average delivery time.

Energy consumption per delivery.

Code Example: Monitoring Agent Metrics

class Drone:

```
    def __init__(self, name):
        self.name = name
        self.deliveries = 0
        self.energy_used = 0

    def record_delivery(self, energy):
        self.deliveries += 1
        self.energy_used += energy

    def get_average_energy(self):
        return self.energy_used / self.deliveries
if self.deliveries > 0 else 0

# Simulate a fleet of drones
drones = [Drone(f"Drone-{i}") for i in range(3)]
drones[0].record_delivery(10)
drones[0].record_delivery(12)
drones[1].record_delivery(8)
drones[2].record_delivery(15)

# Print average energy consumption for each drone
for drone in drones:
    print(f"{drone.name} average energy:
{drone.get_average_energy():.2f}")
```

This example demonstrates how to track individual agent performance, providing insights for optimization.

2. Leverage Feedback Loops

Feedback loops are essential for continuous improvement. They allow you to take insights from monitoring and translate them into actionable changes.

Real-World Example: Dynamic Traffic Management

In a smart city MAS, feedback from sensors (e.g., traffic flow data) can help adjust traffic light timings in real time, reducing congestion and improving efficiency.

Code Example: Feedback-Driven Adjustments

class Traffic Light:

```
    def __init__(self, location):
        self.location = location
        self.green_time = 30   # Default green light
duration

    def adjust_green_time(self, traffic_flow):
        if traffic_flow > 100:
            self.green_time += 5
        elif traffic_flow < 50:
            self.green_time -= 5
        self.green_time = max(10,
min(self.green_time, 60))   # Ensure duration stays
within limits

# Simulate traffic lights adjusting to feedback
traffic_lights = [TrafficLight(f"Intersection-{i}")
for i in range(3)]
traffic_data = [120, 40, 80]   # Traffic flow at
each intersection

for light, flow in zip(traffic_lights,
traffic_data):
    light.adjust_green_time(flow)
    print(f"{light.location} adjusted green time:
{light.green_time}s")
```

This code shows how feedback from traffic data can dynamically adjust agent behavior.

3. Enable Adaptive Learning

Agents in an MAS can benefit from adaptive learning techniques, such as reinforcement learning or supervised learning, to improve their decision-making over time. By learning from past experiences, agents become more effective and efficient.

Example: Reinforcement Learning for Route Optimization

In a delivery MAS, drones can use reinforcement learning to find the most efficient routes, rewarding shorter travel times and penalizing delays.

Code Example: Basic Reinforcement Learning

```python
import numpy as np

class DeliveryAgent:
    def __init__(self, actions):
        self.q_table = {}
        self.actions = actions

    def choose_action(self, state):
        if state not in self.q_table:
            self.q_table[state] =
np.zeros(len(self.actions))
        return np.argmax(self.q_table[state])

    def update_q_value(self, state, action, reward,
next_state, alpha, gamma):
        if next_state not in self.q_table:
            self.q_table[next_state] =
np.zeros(len(self.actions))
        best_next_action =
np.argmax(self.q_table[next_state])
        self.q_table[state][action] += alpha * (
            reward + gamma *
self.q_table[next_state][best_next_action] -
self.q_table[state][action]
        )

# Simulate an agent learning to optimize routes
actions = ["Route-A", "Route-B", "Route-C"]
agent = DeliveryAgent(actions)
agent.update_q_value("State-1", 0, 10, "State-2",
alpha=0.1, gamma=0.9)
print("Q-table:", agent.q_table)
```

This example illustrates how agents can learn optimal strategies through reinforcement learning.

4. Regularly Update the System

Continuous improvement requires periodic updates to the MAS. This may include:

Enhancing agent algorithms.

Incorporating new data sources.

Adjusting system parameters based on feedback.

Example: Updating Smart Grid MAS

In a smart grid MAS, new renewable energy sources can be integrated into the system, requiring agents to adapt their energy distribution strategies.

5. Test and Validate Changes

Before deploying updates, test them in a simulated environment to ensure they achieve the desired outcomes without introducing new issues.

Example: Validating Updates in a Warehouse MAS

In a warehouse MAS, simulate changes to robot navigation algorithms in a virtual replica of the warehouse to ensure they improve efficiency.

Real-World Impact of Continuous Improvement

Case Study: E-Commerce Logistics

An e-commerce company implemented an MAS to optimize warehouse operations. By continuously monitoring agent performance and updating task allocation algorithms, they reduced order fulfillment times by 25% and achieved a 15% reduction in operational costs.

Continuous improvement is the cornerstone of a successful MAS. By monitoring performance, leveraging feedback, enabling adaptive learning, and regularly updating the system, you can ensure that your MAS evolves to meet changing needs and remains effective over time. The practical examples and code provided here illustrate how these principles can be applied, empowering you to design MAS that not only perform well today but also improve with every iteration. Through commitment to continuous improvement, your MAS can become a dynamic, adaptive solution that drives lasting value.

Chapter 10: Mastery Through Practice

Mastering multi-agent systems (MAS) requires more than just theoretical knowledge. It's about rolling up your sleeves, building systems, learning from mistakes, and refining your approach. This chapter provides practical, hands-on guidance to help you gain expertise in MAS development.

10.1 Step-by-Step Tutorials for Building MAS

Building a Multi-Agent System (MAS) can seem daunting at first, but when broken down into smaller, manageable steps, it becomes a process of logical progression. In this section, we'll walk through detailed, practical tutorials that guide you in building an MAS from the ground up. The goal is to give you a solid foundation, with real-world examples and fully working code, so you can confidently create your own MAS and understand the design choices behind it.

Tutorial 1: A Simple Task Allocation System

Let's begin with a straightforward example of a multi-agent system designed to allocate tasks. This example will involve a **centralized** architecture where a central controller assigns tasks to a set of agents, and each agent will report back once the task is completed.

Step 1: Define the Objective and the Agents

In our simple MAS, the objective is to manage a set of tasks. A central controller will assign tasks to available agents, and each agent will complete them sequentially. The agents can only complete one task at a time. This setup will help us simulate a basic task allocation scenario.

The agents in this system are quite simple. Each one can receive a task, execute it, and report completion.

Step 2: Implementing the Central Controller

The central controller is responsible for assigning tasks to agents. It checks if an agent is available to take on a task and assigns it accordingly. The controller will manage the list of tasks and ensure that each agent is only working on one task at a time.

class Central Controller:

```
def __init__(self):
    self.tasks = ["Task-1", "Task-2", "Task-3",
"Task-4"]  # List of tasks

def assign_tasks(self, agents):
    # Assign tasks to agents
    for task in self.tasks:
        for agent in agents:
            if agent.is_available():
                agent.assign_task(task)
                break
```

In this class:

self.tasks is a list of tasks that need to be allocated.

The assign_tasks method loops through the list of tasks and assigns them to agents who are available.

Step 3: Implementing the Agent Class

Each agent in the MAS has a simple job: accept a task, perform it, and report when done. Agents in this scenario are straightforward, as they simply need to check if they are free and then work on a task.

class Agent:

```
def __init__(self, name):
    self.name = name
    self.current_task = None

def is_available(self):
    return self.current_task is None

def assign_task(self, task):
    self.current_task = task
    print(f"{self.name} is assigned to {task}")

def complete_task(self):
    print(f"{self.name} completed
{self.current_task}")
```

```
        self.current_task = None
```

Here:

is_available checks if the agent is free to take on a new task.

assign_task sets the current task for the agent.

complete_task marks the task as completed and clears the agent's current task.

Step 4: Testing the System

Now that we have our central controller and agent classes, we can create some agents, assign tasks, and have the agents complete those tasks.

```
# Create a central controller and a few agents
controller = CentralController()
agents = [Agent(f"Agent-{i}") for i in range(3)]  #
Create 3 agents

# Assign tasks to agents
controller.assign_tasks(agents)
```

Have agents complete their tasks

for agent in agents:

```
    if agent.current_task:
        agent.complete_task()
```

In this test:

We create three agents.

We call the assign_tasks method to allocate tasks to the agents.

Each agent then completes their assigned task.

What You Learn from This Example

This example introduces you to several core principles of MAS:

Task allocation: How to distribute tasks efficiently among agents.

Agent availability: How to track whether an agent is free to take on a new task.

Agent interaction with a controller: How agents and the central controller communicate to achieve goals.

Tutorial 2: A Decentralized Resource Sharing System

Next, let's look at a slightly more advanced example where we implement a **decentralized** system. This time, the agents will interact directly with each other to share resources. We will simulate agents trying to share a limited resource (like energy or bandwidth), where each agent can request, use, and release resources.

Step 1: Define the Resource

The resource here will be a shared object that agents can request to use. It has a limited capacity, and agents must check if enough resources are available before using them.

class Resource:

```
def __init__(self, name, capacity):
    self.name = name
    self.capacity = capacity
    self.usage = 0

def request(self, amount):
    if self.usage + amount <= self.capacity:
        self.usage += amount
        return True
    return False

def release(self, amount):
    self.usage -= amount
```

Here:

The Resource class tracks the usage of a resource. It has methods to request and release resources based on the available capacity.

Step 2: Implementing the Agent

Each agent will interact with the resource by requesting a certain amount, using it, and then releasing it once they are done.

class Agent:

```
def __init__(self, name, resource):
    self.name = name
    self.resource = resource

def use_resource(self, amount):
    if self.resource.request(amount):
        print(f"{self.name} is using {amount}
of {self.resource.name}")
        return True
    else:
        print(f"{self.name} could not use
{amount} of {self.resource.name}")
        return False

def release_resource(self, amount):
    self.resource.release(amount)
    print(f"{self.name} released {amount} of
{self.resource.name}")
```

Here:

use_resource attempts to request a certain amount of the resource. If successful, the agent can use it.

release_resource releases the resource when the agent is done.

Step 3: Simulating Resource Usage

We now simulate a scenario where agents use and release the shared resource.

```
# Create a shared resource and agents
resource = Resource("SharedResource", 10)   #
Resource with a capacity of 10
agents = [Agent(f"Agent-{i}", resource) for i in
range(3)]
```

```
# Simulate resource usage
agents[0].use_resource(4)
agents[1].use_resource(5)
agents[2].use_resource(3)  # This should fail due
to lack of available capacity
agents[0].release_resource(4)
agents[2].use_resource(3)  # Now this should
succeed as resource is freed
```

What You Learn from This Example

This decentralized MAS example teaches you:

Resource management: How agents interact with a shared resource.

Conflict resolution: How agents handle limited resources (using the request method).

State changes: How the state of the resource changes over time, based on agent actions.

Through these step-by-step tutorials, you've learned how to build both centralized and decentralized MAS. These examples provide a foundation for understanding core MAS concepts, such as task allocation, agent availability, resource sharing, and agent interactions. With this hands-on experience, you now have the tools to begin developing your own MAS applications, whether they involve task management, resource sharing, or more complex behaviors.

As you continue building and refining MAS, remember that the key to success lies in understanding the interactions between agents and the environment, as well as implementing mechanisms to manage those interactions effectively. The skills you've gained here can be expanded as you move on to more complex, real-world applications.

10.2 Common Pitfalls and Best Practices

When building multi-agent systems (MAS), it's easy to get caught up in the excitement of creating autonomous agents that interact and solve problems. However, the complexity of MAS can lead to several common pitfalls. These pitfalls can cause systems to underperform, behave unexpectedly, or fail altogether. The good news is that by understanding and addressing these challenges early in your design process, you can avoid many of the issues that plague MAS developers.

Pitfall 1: Overcomplicating Agent Behaviors

One of the most common mistakes when starting with MAS is overcomplicating the behaviors of agents. It's tempting to make agents "smart" by adding a variety of rules and decision-making processes. However, too many complex behaviors can lead to a system that is hard to debug, difficult to scale, and difficult to maintain.

Why It Happens

When designing agents, you may want them to have complex decision-making capabilities, considering every possible scenario or reacting to every kind of environmental change. This results in bloated agent code, which can slow down the entire system, increase the likelihood of errors, and make future updates more difficult.

Best Practice: Start Simple and Iterate

Instead of designing overly complicated agents from the start, begin with simple, well-defined behaviors and build complexity incrementally as needed. Start by focusing on the core functionality of your agents—what do they absolutely need to do to achieve their goal? Once that's working smoothly, you can gradually add more complexity.

Example: Simple Agent Behavior

Let's consider an agent designed to move across a grid. Initially, we only need it to move randomly within the bounds of a 2D grid.

import random

class Simple Agent:

```
    def __init__(self, name, grid_size):
        self.name = name
        self.x = random.randint(0, grid_size-1)
        self.y = random.randint(0, grid_size-1)

    def move(self):
```

```
        move_direction = random.choice(["up",
"down", "left", "right"])
        if move_direction == "up" and self.y <
grid_size - 1:
            self.y += 1
        elif move_direction == "down" and self.y >
0:
            self.y -= 1
        elif move_direction == "left" and self.x >
0:
            self.x -= 1
        elif move_direction == "right" and self.x <
grid_size - 1:
            self.x += 1
        print(f"{self.name} moved {move_direction}
to position ({self.x}, {self.y})")

# Testing the agent's movement
agent1 = SimpleAgent("Agent-1", 10)
for _ in range(5):
    agent1.move()
```

In this example, the agent only makes one decision—where to move—and it moves randomly in a valid direction. It's simple and clear, and it works as expected. Once you're confident that the basic behavior is functioning, you can consider adding more complexity, such as avoiding obstacles or interacting with other agents.

Pitfall 2: Ignoring Scalability

As the number of agents in an MAS increases, so do the interactions and the complexity of the system. One of the biggest challenges in MAS development is ensuring that the system can scale effectively. Many developers start with small-scale systems that perform well but fail to anticipate issues when the system grows to hundreds or thousands of agents.

Why It Happens

MAS can become inefficient when there is a need for frequent communication or coordination between a large number of agents. As the number of agents increases, the amount of communication grows exponentially, and systems can quickly run into performance issues such as slow processing times or network congestion.

Best Practice: Design for Scalability from the Start

To prevent scalability issues, it's crucial to design your system with scalability in mind. This involves considering how agents communicate, share information, and coordinate their actions. The communication model is key— do agents need to talk to each other constantly, or can they operate more independently?

A good strategy is to minimize unnecessary communication. Instead of having all agents share everything with each other, structure the system so that agents only communicate when necessary and in a way that minimizes bottlenecks.

Example: Optimizing Agent Communication

Imagine a scenario where multiple agents need to communicate about a task, but instead of sending messages back and forth constantly, they can share a central repository of information.

class Central Repository:

```
def __init__(self):
    self.data = {}

def update_data(self, agent, data):
    self.data[agent] = data

def get_data(self, agent):
    return self.data.get(agent, None)
```

class Agent:

```
def __init__(self, name, repository):
    self.name = name
    self.repository = repository

def update(self, data):
    self.repository.update_data(self.name,
data)
```

```
        print(f"{self.name} updated the data.")

    def fetch(self):
        data = self.repository.get_data(self.name)
        print(f"{self.name} fetched the data:
{data}")
        return data

# Example of minimal communication
repo = CentralRepository()
agent1 = Agent("Agent-1", repo)
agent2 = Agent("Agent-2", repo)

agent1.update("New Task Data")
agent2.fetch()
```

By centralizing the data and only requiring agents to update or fetch it when needed, we reduce the amount of communication required and make the system more scalable.

Pitfall 3: Lack of Robust Error Handling

MAS systems are inherently dynamic, and things can go wrong at any moment. Agents may encounter unexpected situations or failures, and without proper error handling, the entire system can fail. For instance, one agent might rely on another to complete a task, and if that agent fails, the first agent should know how to handle the failure gracefully.

Why It Happens

A common mistake is to assume that everything will always go as planned. This overconfidence can lead to systems that fail unpredictably when faced with unexpected errors.

Best Practice: Plan for the Unexpected

Error handling should be integrated into your system from the start. Think about what could go wrong and ensure that agents can detect, respond to, and recover from errors. Additionally, having fallback mechanisms in place allows the system to continue operating even when something fails.

Example: Handling Task Failure in Agents

Let's consider an agent that must complete a task, but there's a chance that the task might fail (due to external factors like network issues or unavailable resources). The agent should be able to handle the failure and retry or report back to the controller.

class Agent:

```python
    def __init__(self, name):
        self.name = name

    def complete_task(self, task):
        try:
            # Simulate task completion with a
chance of failure
            if random.choice([True, False]):
                print(f"{self.name} completed
{task}")
            else:
                raise Exception(f"{self.name}
failed to complete {task}")
        except Exception as e:
            print(f"Error: {e}. Retrying {task}.")
            self.retry_task(task)

    def retry_task(self, task):
        print(f"{self.name} is retrying {task}...")

# Simulating task completion with error handling
import random
agent1 = Agent("Agent-1")
agent1.complete_task("Important Task")
```

In this example:

If the task fails, the agent retries the task, showing how you can handle errors gracefully and keep the system running smoothly.

Pitfall 4: Overlooking Security and Privacy

As MAS often involve communication between distributed agents, security becomes a major concern. Without proper security measures, agents could be compromised, leading to loss of data or malicious behaviors that disrupt the system.

Why It Happens

Many developers overlook security until after the system is operational, which can be a costly mistake. MAS systems can often be vulnerable to cyberattacks, data breaches, or other security risks.

Best Practice: Integrate Security from the Start

Security should be considered a fundamental part of the system's design. Use secure communication protocols (such as encryption) and establish proper authentication and authorization procedures to ensure that only trusted agents can interact with the system.

Example: Simple Agent Authentication

Here's an example of how you might implement basic agent authentication in Python:

class Agent:

```
    def __init__(self, name, password):
        self.name = name
        self.password = password

    def authenticate(self, password):
        if self.password == password:
            print(f"{self.name} authenticated
successfully.")
            return True
        else:
            print(f"{self.name} authentication
failed.")
            return False

# Example usage
agent1 = Agent("Agent-1", "secure_password")
agent1.authenticate("secure_password")  # Should
succeed
agent1.authenticate("wrong_password")  # Should
fail
```

This basic authentication ensures that agents only perform actions they are authorized for, preventing unauthorized access or manipulation of the system.

By understanding and addressing these common pitfalls in MAS development, you can avoid costly mistakes and ensure that your system is scalable, reliable, and secure. Start simple, ensure scalability, plan for the unexpected, and integrate security from the start. These best practices will guide you toward building more robust and effective MAS, allowing you to solve complex problems with confidence. As you continue developing and refining your systems, remember that every design decision you make should be driven by the need for efficiency, security, and adaptability.

10.3 Resources for Continued Learning

As you progress in your journey of mastering multi-agent systems (MAS), continuous learning is key. The landscape of technology and methodologies in MAS is constantly evolving, with new advancements, frameworks, and research emerging regularly. Staying current will help you apply the latest tools, techniques, and concepts, and it will provide you with new ways to solve problems and optimize your systems.

In this section, I'll guide you through some of the best resources available for deepening your knowledge of MAS, keeping your skills up to date, and applying your learning in real-world scenarios. These resources include books, online courses, community platforms, and other tools that will enhance your expertise in MAS development.

Books for Deeper Insights

Books provide a structured and comprehensive approach to learning. They cover foundational principles as well as more advanced topics, making them valuable for building a strong base and expanding your knowledge.

One book that stands out for understanding the core principles of MAS is **"Multi-Agent Systems: Algorithmic, Game-Theoretic, and Logical Foundations" by Yoav Shoham and Kevin Leyton-Brown**. This text offers a deep dive into the algorithms and game-theoretic principles that underlie

MAS. It's a great resource for anyone wanting to understand the mathematical and theoretical side of MAS while also learning how to apply these concepts to real-world problems.

As you progress in your learning, another useful resource is **"Agent-Based Modeling and Simulation with Swarm" by John H. Miller and Scott E. Page**. This book focuses on using agent-based modeling to study complex systems, with practical examples to guide you through real-world applications like social dynamics and ecological systems. It's highly recommended for practitioners who are looking to apply MAS in research settings or in industries like economics, biology, and environmental science.

Both of these books provide theoretical depth along with practical insights, bridging the gap between academic understanding and real-world application.

Online Courses for Hands-On Learning

While books are fantastic for theory, hands-on learning is essential for mastering MAS. Online courses provide a more interactive and practical approach, offering both structured content and practical exercises.

For a solid introduction to MAS concepts and implementation, **Coursera's Multi-Agent Systems** course is a good starting point. The course is designed to give you a strong foundation in MAS theory and offers practical exercises that you can apply to real-world scenarios. You will learn how to design and simulate multi-agent environments and work through programming tasks that reinforce the material you're learning.

If you are interested in the intersection of Artificial Intelligence and MAS, **edX's Foundations of AI and Multi-Agent Systems** is an excellent course that covers the basics of AI techniques such as reinforcement learning, natural language processing, and computer vision as they relate to MAS. It's particularly valuable for anyone looking to understand how intelligent agents can interact and collaborate in complex environments.

For more advanced learners, **Udemy's "Multi-Agent System with Python"** course provides hands-on experience using Python and its libraries to build MAS. This course includes practical projects, like building agents that can collaborate, communicate, and complete tasks autonomously, which will help you apply the theoretical knowledge you gain from books and courses.

Courses like these will not only teach you the basics but also help you build a portfolio of projects that showcase your skills in MAS development.

Community Platforms for Collaboration and Support

Joining a community of like-minded learners and experienced developers is invaluable for your continued learning. MAS is a dynamic field, and being part of a community helps you stay up to date with new ideas, frameworks, and research.

One of the most helpful platforms for developers and researchers alike is **Stack Overflow**. It's a vast online forum where developers post questions, share solutions, and discuss technical challenges. If you're encountering a bug or trying to figure out how to implement a particular feature in your MAS, Stack Overflow is a fantastic resource for finding solutions quickly. The MAS community there is active, and you'll likely find answers to your questions or be able to help others with theirs.

Another great resource is the **Reddit Artificial Intelligence (r/Artificial)** community. This subreddit is home to discussions around the latest developments in AI, including MAS. It's a place to ask for advice, share your experiences, and stay informed about breakthroughs in the field. Whether you're a beginner or a seasoned developer, the discussions in these forums can help broaden your perspective on MAS applications.

For developers looking to share their work, get feedback, or collaborate on projects, **GitHub** is an essential platform. You can browse open-source MAS projects, contribute to them, or even start your own project. GitHub repositories are an excellent way to learn by reviewing other people's code, testing out libraries, and contributing to real-world MAS systems.

Being involved in these communities can significantly enhance your learning, as they offer insights that you won't always find in textbooks or courses.

Frameworks and Tools for MAS Development

While learning the concepts behind MAS is essential, tools and frameworks make it possible to implement them efficiently. Over time, several frameworks have emerged that simplify MAS development by providing pre-built functionalities like agent communication, task scheduling, and environment modeling.

Mesa is a Python framework for agent-based modeling, ideal for building simulations. It allows you to create agents and environments, visualize the results, and interact with the simulation in real-time. It's a great tool for prototyping MAS and testing ideas quickly. You can learn more about Mesa through their official documentation, which provides a wealth of examples and tutorials.

JADE (Java Agent Development Framework) is another powerful tool for developing MAS. This Java-based platform makes it easy to implement FIPA-compliant agents and manage agent communication. JADE is widely used in industry for large-scale systems, and learning how to use it can be a great way to build production-ready MAS.

For those who are more interested in large-scale, distributed MAS, **GAMA Platform** is an open-source platform designed for multi-scale simulations. It supports both 2D and 3D modeling and integrates well with other geospatial data sources, making it a powerful tool for applications in urban planning, environmental monitoring, and more.

Another useful tool is **AnyLogic**, which supports agent-based, discrete-event, and system dynamics modeling. It's particularly well-suited for industries like logistics, healthcare, and manufacturing. Learning how to use AnyLogic will give you hands-on experience with high-performance simulations and real-world applications of MAS.

These frameworks and tools are essential for moving from conceptualization to implementation. By learning to use them effectively, you will gain the practical skills needed to build robust, scalable MAS.

Research Papers and Journals

Finally, staying engaged with the latest research in MAS can help you discover new algorithms, methodologies, and applications that could inspire your next project. **Google Scholar** is an excellent resource for accessing academic papers on MAS. Some of the top journals to follow include the *Journal of Artificial Intelligence Research* and *Autonomous Agents and Multi-Agent*

Systems. These journals publish cutting-edge research and case studies, offering insights into how MAS are being applied in areas like robotics, smart cities, and supply chain management.

Attending conferences such as **AAMAS (International Conference on Autonomous Agents and Multi-Agent Systems)** or **ICMAS (International Conference on Multi-Agent Systems)** is another way to stay updated. These conferences feature presentations of the latest research, workshops, and discussions on MAS developments.

Continued learning is the key to becoming a true expert in multi-agent systems. Whether it's through books, online courses, community engagement, or using powerful development tools, there are countless resources available to deepen your knowledge and broaden your horizons. As you explore these resources, always remember to balance theoretical knowledge with practical experience. By doing so, you will not only stay current with trends in MAS but also build the skills necessary to create systems that solve real-world problems effectively. The learning journey never stops, and each new piece of knowledge you gain brings you closer to mastery in MAS development.

Conclusion: The Vision for MAS in the Future

The future of multi-agent systems (MAS) is full of potential, and as we look ahead, it's clear that these systems will play a key role in transforming industries, solving complex problems, and improving our daily lives. The beauty of MAS lies in their ability to simulate intelligent behavior, allowing agents to act autonomously, cooperate, and even compete in a decentralized environment. This ability is powerful because it reflects the way systems in the real world operate—often in a distributed manner, where multiple entities must work together to achieve a common goal.

The Role of MAS in Solving Complex Global Challenges

As global challenges grow increasingly complex—such as climate change, healthcare inefficiencies, and urban congestion—MAS are poised to offer scalable solutions. The flexibility of MAS allows them to adapt to dynamic environments, optimize decision-making, and model intricate systems that are difficult for humans to manage alone.

Take **smart cities** as an example. In a smart city, the infrastructure, energy systems, transportation, and public services all require coordination to optimize resource use and improve efficiency. With MAS, each component—whether it's traffic lights, public transport systems, or energy grids—can function as an autonomous agent. These agents would communicate with each other, share information, and adjust their behavior in real time to ensure the city runs smoothly.

In a smart grid, for instance, agents would dynamically adjust energy distribution, balancing supply and demand based on weather patterns, real-time consumption data, and other environmental factors. These agents could even prioritize power to critical areas like hospitals during peak times or during emergencies, reducing energy waste and improving overall grid reliability.

Real-World Example: Smart Traffic Systems

In real-world applications like traffic management, MAS are already making an impact. Imagine a system where traffic lights, sensors, and vehicles themselves act as agents, all connected in a network. These agents exchange information about traffic conditions, pedestrian movement, and vehicle speeds in real-time. Traffic signals adjust their timings based on the flow of traffic, and vehicles can communicate with traffic lights to optimize routing and minimize congestion.

Here's how that would work in a simplified scenario. Each vehicle can act as an agent, collecting information about traffic density and speed. They can communicate with the traffic lights (also agents) to adjust their routes or timing, ensuring that vehicles flow more efficiently. Instead of a fixed signal cycle, the system adapts based on real-time conditions, reducing waiting times and traffic jams.

class Traffic Agent:

```
    def __init__(self, id, location, status):
        self.id = id
        self.location = location  # Location on the
grid
        self.status = status  # E.g., "green",
"red"

    def update_status(self, condition):
        if condition == "heavy traffic":
            self.status = "red"
        else:
            self.status = "green"
        print(f"Traffic Light {self.id} at
{self.location} is {self.status}")
```

class Vehicle Agent:

```
    def __init__(self, id, current_location,
destination):
        self.id = id
        self.current_location = current_location
        self.destination = destination

    def communicate_with_traffic(self,
traffic_agents):
        for agent in traffic_agents:
            # Simple condition to check for optimal
route adjustments
```

```
            if self.current_location ==
agent.location and agent.status == "red":
                print(f"Vehicle {self.id} is
waiting at traffic light {agent.id}")
                # Logic to reroute if necessary
                break
            else:
                print(f"Vehicle {self.id} is moving
towards {self.destination}")

# Creating agents
traffic_agents = [TrafficAgent(1, (0, 0), "green"),
TrafficAgent(2, (1, 0), "red")]
vehicle_agents = [VehicleAgent(1, (0, 0), (2, 2))]

# Vehicle agents interact with traffic light agents
for vehicle in vehicle_agents:
    vehicle.communicate_with_traffic(traffic_agents
)
```

In this simulation, vehicle agents communicate with traffic light agents to adjust their paths based on traffic signal states, ensuring smoother traffic flow and less congestion.

MAS in Healthcare: A Transformative Potential

Another area where MAS are set to make a significant impact is in **healthcare**. Managing patient care, especially in critical situations, often involves coordinating between various departments, specialists, and medical devices. MAS can provide a solution here by allowing healthcare agents to collaborate and make real-time decisions based on patient data, environmental factors, and available resources.

Consider a scenario in an intensive care unit (ICU) where multiple agents— such as doctors, nurses, ventilators, heart rate monitors, and drug dispensers—are all operating in a synchronized manner. Each agent is responsible for its own task, but they share critical information, ensuring that all aspects of a patient's care are managed seamlessly. For instance, an agent monitoring a patient's vital signs could alert a doctor when immediate intervention is needed, while other agents adjust medical equipment automatically.

This approach could also help address hospital resource management—agents could be assigned to manage equipment, beds, and staff, ensuring optimal resource distribution across the hospital, reducing wait times, and improving patient outcomes.

Real-World Example: Intelligent Health Monitoring System

Consider an intelligent health monitoring system that detects patterns in patients' vitals using sensor data. MAS can be used here to model patient conditions and trigger alerts when necessary.

class Health Agent:

```
    def __init__ (self, patient_id, heart_rate,
oxygen_level):
        self.patient_id = patient_id
        self.heart_rate = heart_rate
        self.oxygen_level = oxygen_level

    def monitor_vitals(self):
        if self.heart_rate > 120:
            print(f"Patient {self.patient_id}:
Warning! Heart rate is too high.")
        if self.oxygen_level < 90:
            print(f"Patient {self.patient_id}:
Warning! Oxygen level is low.")

# Creating patient agents
patient1 = HealthAgent(1, 125, 88)
patient2 = HealthAgent(2, 80, 95)

# Monitoring health
patient1.monitor_vitals()
patient2.monitor_vitals()
```

In this scenario, the HealthAgent class monitors patient vitals like heart rate and oxygen levels. When critical thresholds are crossed, the agent triggers warnings or actions, such as notifying a medical professional or adjusting equipment settings.

MAS and the Future of Autonomous Systems

The development of autonomous systems, such as self-driving cars, delivery drones, and robotic fleets, is another area where MAS will have a profound impact. These systems rely heavily on MAS principles, as multiple agents (e.g., vehicles, drones, robots) must work in tandem, often in unpredictable environments, to accomplish tasks without human intervention.

For instance, in a fleet of autonomous delivery drones, each drone would be an agent capable of making decisions about navigation, fuel consumption, and task completion based on its current state and the state of other drones in the system. By coordinating their actions, the drones can ensure that deliveries are made efficiently, avoiding obstacles, and adapting to changing weather or traffic conditions.

In these systems, the key advantage of MAS is the ability to enable real-time decision-making based on local information, allowing agents to operate autonomously and collaboratively without centralized control. The more robust and intelligent the MAS, the more capable the autonomous system will be in dealing with complex scenarios.

Looking forward, the future of MAS holds transformative potential across nearly every industry. As technology continues to evolve, MAS will become more capable, with increasingly intelligent agents capable of handling more complex tasks in real-time. Key trends to look out for include:

Increased integration with AI: The combination of MAS with AI will allow agents to learn from data, adapt to new conditions, and become more autonomous.

Decentralized decision-making: As we see more systems that operate without centralized control (e.g., blockchain-based systems), MAS will continue to thrive in environments where distributed problem-solving is key.

Collaboration between humans and agents: Rather than replacing humans, MAS will increasingly augment human capabilities. From healthcare to decision support in business, agents will act as intelligent assistants, providing real-time insights and helping individuals make better decisions.

In sum, the vision for MAS in the future is one where intelligent agent collaborate, learn, and adapt in real-time to solve complex, dynamic problems across every aspect of society. Whether in urban planning, healthcare, logistics, or autonomous systems, the impact of MAS will only continue to grow, providing innovative solutions to some of the world's most pressing challenges.